MOLL FLANDERS

The Making of a Criminal Mind

TWAYNE'S MASTERWORK STUDIES
Robert Lecker, General Editor

MOLL FLANDERS

The Making of a Criminal Mind

PAULA R. BACKSCHEIDER

Twayne Publishers • Boston
A Division of G. K. Hall & Co.

Moll Flanders: The Making of a Criminal Mind
Paula R. Backscheider

Twayne's Masterwork Studies No. 48
Copyright 1990 by G. K. Hall & Co.
All rights reserved.
Published by Twayne Publishers
A division of G. K. Hall & Co.
70 Lincoln Street, Boston, Massachusetts 02111

Copyediting supervised by Barbara Sutton.
Book production by Gabrielle B. McDonald.
Typeset by Compositors Corporation, Cedar Rapids, Iowa.

Printed on permanent/durable acid-free paper
and bound in the United States of America.

Library of Congress Cataloging-in-Publication Data

Backscheider, Paula R.
    Moll Flanders : the making of a criminal mind / Paula
Backscheider.
        p.   cm. — (Twayne's masterwork studies ; no. 48)
    Includes bibliographical references.
    1. Defoe, Daniel, 1661?–1731. Fortunes and misfortunes of the
famous Moll Flanders.   2. Criminals in literature.   I. Title.
II. Series.
PR3404.F653B3   1990
823'.5–dc20   89–29597
                                                                    CIP

First printing 1990
0-8057-9429-8   10 9 8 7 6 5 4 3 2 1
0-8057-8130-7 (pbk.)   10 9 8 7 6 5 4 3 2 1

Contents

Note on the References and Acknowledgments

The best teaching edition of *Moll Flanders* is probably the Penguin Classic, edited by David Blewitt (London, 1989). It reprints the first edition, glosses words when modern meanings differ significantly, has a helpful introduction and useful notes, and even includes three maps (of London, of the Smithfield Market area, and of the Chesapeake territory). Because this edition was not published until this book was in press, I have used G. A. Starr's edition (1971; reprint, New York: Oxford University Press, 1984). Like Starr's edition, J. Paul Hunter's *Moll Flanders* (New York: Crowell, 1970) is carefully edited and has helpful, admirably researched notes; unfortunately, it is out of print, and Starr's is available only in hard cover. Other editions have inferior notes or print the shorter, probably unauthorized, third edition.

I am grateful to the University of Rochester for the reproduction of the frontispiece portrait of Defoe.

The portrait of Defoe published with his *True Collection of the Writings of the Author of the True-Born Englishman* (1703).

Chronology: Daniel Defoe's Life and Works

1658	Oliver Cromwell, lord protector, dies 3 September and is succeeded by his son Richard.
1659	Richard Cromwell resigns 25 May.
1660	Convention Parliament invites Charles II to return to England on 25 April. Daniel Defoe probably born in the autumn, the son of James Foe, a London tallow chandler, and his wife, Alice.
1662	Nonconformist clergy ejected from their churches on 24 August by the Act of Uniformity; among other things, the act required clergymen to assent to everything in the Book of Common Prayer, which some had not had the opportunity to see.
1665	The Plague strikes London; more than 97,000 die.
1666	War between England and France breaks out. The Great Fire of London breaks out on 2 September; 13,000 houses burned.
1667	Milton's *Paradise Lost* published.
1674–1678?	Studies at Charles Morton's Newington Green Academy, a school for Nonconformists that earned a great reputation.
1681	Decides not to go into the Nonconformist ministry.
1681–1692	Is a hose factor and an investor in import/export trade and in such things as a diving bell and civet cats.
1684	On 1 January marries Mary Tuffley, daughter of a wealthy cooper, who brings him a large dowry, £3700.
1685	Charles II dies 6 February and is succeeded by James II. Monmouth rebels 11 June and Defoe joins his army.

Monmouth is defeated at Sedgemoor 6 July. Defoe manages to escape being captured.

1688   The Glorious Revolution. William of Orange is invited to England, and James II flees to France.

1689   William and Mary crowned.

1692   Bankrupt and imprisoned for debt in the Fleet Prison on 29 October and again on 4 November.

1693   Imprisoned for debt in the King's Bench Prison on 12 February; negotiates terms with his creditors; begins to work for Thomas Neale as a manager-trustee for Neale's private lotteries.

1695   Becomes an accountant to one of the commissioners of the Glass Duty and proprietor of a brick and tile works in Essex.

1697   *An Essay upon Projects,* his first long work.

1701   *The True-Born Englishman,* one of the most popular poems of the century; it ridicules those who resented King William because he was Dutch. After this time, sometimes signed his published works "By the Author of *The True-Born Englishman.*"

1702   King William dies 19 March after a fall from his horse, and Anne, a strong supporter of the Church of England, comes to the throne. The Bill to Prevent Occasional Conformity—legislature intended to bar Nonconformists like Defoe from public office and to restrict other civil rights—is introduced into Parliament. *The Shortest Way with the Dissenters,* a satire of Anglican High Church severity toward the Nonconformists, is published.

1703   *The Shortest Way with the Dissenters* is declared a seditious libel, ordered burned by the Common Hangman, and a warrant for Defoe's arrest is sworn out. Defoe is captured 21 May at the home of a Spittlefields weaver and is imprisoned in Newgate. On 5 June he is released on bail.

1703   Convicted of seditious libel 7 July and sentenced to stand in the pillory three times, pay a fine of 200 marks, and find sureties for good behavior for seven years. Released from

Newgate Prison 8 November through Robert Harley's intercessions; is bankrupt again.

1704	First issue of the *Review,* his essay periodical, published 19 February.
1704	Begins traveling through the south and east of England for Secretary of State Robert Harley in the summer; samples public opinion and identifies important men and issues for Harley.
1705	Travels throughout England for Harley July through November.
1706	Goes to Scotland 13 September to work for the union between England and Scotland, which are separate countries. Has been able to make new arrangements with his creditors and expects to be issued a Commission of Bankruptcy, which will protect him from future prosecutions.
1708	Robert Harley forced out of office 11 February. Defoe begins working for Lord Treasurer Sidney Godolphin.
1709	*History of the Union of Scotland and England.*
1709	On 5 November the Reverend Henry Sacheverell preaches an inflammatory sermon that challenges the idea of a parliamentary monarchy established at the time of William's accession. Parliament votes to impeach him.
1710	Sacheverell convicted 20 March, but his light sentence is tantamount to a victory. With the Tory triumph, Harley returns to power. Defoe resumes working for Harley.
1713	England negotiates a separate peace with France in order to end the War of Spanish Succession. Some of England's allies refuse to sign the treaty and continue to fight. Defoe arrested for debt 23 March and spends 11 days in prison; arrested for seditious libel 11 April and taken to Newgate where he spends a weekend. The charges are trumped up by an enemy who persuaded the government to prosecute him for three ironic pamphlets as if they were to be read literally. Committed to the Queen's Bench Prison for contempt of court on 22 April after publishing an outraged account of his arrest.

	He publishes apologies in the 28 April and 5 May *Reviews*, pays a token fine, and is released.
1713–1714	Defends the separate peace, the treaty, and Harley's policies.
1714	Many Englishmen enraged over clauses in the Treaty of Commerce and Navigation that give the French most favored nation status at the expense of some former English allies, including Portugal. Defoe continues to defend the treaty.
1714	Queen Anne dies 1 August. George I, Elector of Hanover and one of the Allies who refused to endorse the separate peace, becomes King of England. Defoe indicted 3 September for seditious libel for implying that one of George's regents was a Jacobite.
1715	In exchange for the end of the prosecution, begins to work for Secretary of State Townshend, primarily as a journalist, in November. Harley indicted for high treason and sent to the Tower. Defoe continues to defend him in print. The Jacobite rebellion. On 6 September the Earl of Mar raises the Pretender's flag; on 22 December the Pretender lands at Peterhead, but on 4 February 1716 he returns to France. During and after the Rebellion, Defoe writes extensively against the Jacobites. *The Family Instructor,* the first of his conduct books and a popular book into the nineteenth century, is published.
1717	Begins to write for Mist's *Weekly Journal.*
1719	*Robinson Crusoe* published in April. Four editions sell out before its sequel, *Farther Adventures of Robinson Crusoe,* is published in August.
1720	The South Sea Company stock increases astronomically in value and then falls (from a high of over £1,000 in June to £180 in September). *Memoirs of a Cavalier* and *Captain Singleton* published.
1722	Novels *Moll Flanders, A Journal of the Plague Year,* and *Colonel Jack* appear.
1722	Invests in land in Essex, begins farming, and tries to start a new brick and tile factory.
1724	Last novel, *The Fortunate Mistress,* or, as it is called today,

	Roxana, and the first volume of *A Tour thro' the Whole Island of Great Britain* published.
1724	Defoe's Colchester, Essex, partner, John Ward, begins court action against him for unpaid debts.
1725	First volume of *The Complete English Tradesman* published.
1726	Swift publishes *Gulliver's Travels* and Defoe the third volume of his *Tour thro' the Whole Island of Great Britain.*
1727	George I dies 10 June; George II and Caroline crowned on 11 October.
1728	Mary Brooke and Elizabeth Stancliffe begin a suit against Defoe over an old debt. John Gay's *Beggar's Opera* is first performed 29 January, and on 18 May the first edition of Alexander Pope's *Dunciad* appears. Defoe's *A Plan of the English Commerce* is published; twenty-two years after his death, it is still described as "an esteemed Work."
1730	Loses court case to Mary Brooke, who had charged that he had never paid a £400 debt and that it was now owed to the estate she had inherited. Goes into hiding to avoid imprisonment for debt.
1731	Dies 24 April of a lethargy, what is now called a stroke, in lodgings on Rope-Makers Alley in the City of London.
1731	Buried 26 April in Bunhill Fields, the famous cemetery for Dissenters.
1732	Mary Defoe is buried 19 December in Bunhill Fields.

CHAPTER
1

Historical
Context

When Daniel Defoe wrote *Moll Flanders* he was sixty-two years old and had been what we would call a journalist for eighteen years. He had written about almost every political, religious, economic, and social issue, and *Moll Flanders* exemplifies fully his engagement with his own time.

Moll Flanders reflects the economic problems of the first decades of the eighteenth century. Although Moll dramatizes the particular difficulties of women, it is not she alone who finds making a living difficult. One of Moll's husbands goes broke, another loses a sum of money he loaned and dies in despair, and another, like so many of his countrymen, is forced to emigrate. Defoe, a proponent of aggressive colonization since the 1690s, used this novel, *Robinson Crusoe,* and *Colonel Jack* to suggest that the New World, not London, offered young people the opportunities they sought. The movement of the population into the cities as the rural economy faltered meant that waves of unskilled, naive men and women became the victims and then the perpetrators of crime. In Defoe's youth, almost every person in a parish or even a ward was known by everyone else. Now the criminal could fade into the amorphous crowd. A man or woman could be assaulted and robbed in daylight on a London street and the thief never identified. Strangers moving through the crowded neighborhoods attracted no attention.

Moll Flanders is, of course, a novel about a criminal, and crime was very much on the minds of English people in 1720. In fact, they believed they were in the midst of an unprecedented crime wave. The so-called Black Act that was passed in 1723, the year after the publication of Moll Flanders, included the most extensive increase in the number of offenses classified as capital instituted in that century.

With the growing concern over crime came greater interest in criminals. The weekly journals increased their coverage of crime and joined the sessions papers, broadsides, the Newgate Ordinary's Account, pamphlet lives, and collections such as Alexander Smith's A Compleat History of the Lives and Robberies of the Most Notorious Highway-Men, Footpads, Shop-Lifts, and Cheats, of Both Sexes. Always alert to what his contemporaries were interested in and eager to analyze, explain, and point out the implications of social change, Defoe began to publish extensively on crime and criminals. Applebee's Journal, a paper to which Defoe probably contributed, specialized in the lives and trials of pirates and felons. The fact that such books by Defoe and others sold well shows that the subject matter of Moll Flanders was of intense interest to his contemporaries.

Moll is like these new criminals—a country girl in London. Her first crime, the impetuous theft of a bundle momentarily left unattended, probably duplicated the crimes of many young men and women unable to support themselves in the city. Her descent into the heart of the London underworld provided Defoe's readers with a tour of London life many heard about but never saw. As Moll steals watches in every conceivable way, snatches whatever silver she can find lying about, and schemes to make off with bolts of expensive (and sometimes contraband) cloth, she offers people a guide to protecting their possessions. Her few sexual adventures suggest how easily women could slide into prostitution, the other criminal activity that claimed so many girls in London and other cities. In fact, some scholars have asserted that Moll is a composite of several real criminals, particularly Moll King and Callico Sarah.[1]

Defoe was a man with great sensitivity to injustice and insatiable curiosity about causes and origins. The father of six daughters (four surviving), Defoe himself had been in prison several times. His understanding of woman's situation was acute, and his view of law-breakers far from simple-minded. Neither sentimental nor unforgiving, he habitually sketched the forces that inclined them toward crime, and these included broken homes, negligent parents, poor education, bad company, and youthful mistakes. *Moll Flanders* includes many elements of the popular, formulaic criminal lives. Criminal lives usually sketched in the background of the subject, often included something about childhood, described each crime in some detail, and then described the capture, the trial, and (usually) the death of the criminal. Not only did Defoe include these things and draw upon his own experiences and work as a reporter, but he included elements of his conduct books and "projects" (the eighteenth-century term for schemes for improvements). His books of this kind had titles such as *An Essay upon Projects, Religious Courtship,* and *An Effectual Scheme for the Immediate Preventing of Street Robberies* and presented his ideas on a number of subjects raised in *Moll Flanders.* His conduct books, for instance, endlessly cautioned young girls about the pitfalls of courtship, and his projects called for younger, more able-bodied watchmen, better street lights, and a new system of getting witnesses to testify.

Another aspect of the historical context of *Moll Flanders* is, of course, literary. People enjoyed fiction as never before, and longer forms of it were rapidly becoming popular. Defoe's own *Robinson Crusoe* (1719) had been a best-seller, and writers who imitated it remarked that it represented the taste for "histories at large." By this term, Defoe's contemporaries meant long, somewhat unified stories that concentrated on a character's interior life, introduced other interesting characters, and built the plot on fairly complicated decisions. These novels were increasingly set at least partly in London, as opposed to the exotic, faraway settings of fiction of the Restoration. Novels such as Mary Hearne's *The Female Deserters* (1719) and Penelope Aubin's *The Life of Madame de Beaumont* (1721) as well as thick collections such as Alexander Smith's *The Secret History of the Lives of the most celebrated Beauties . . . and Jilts from Fair Rosamond down to this Present Age* (1715) suggest the expanding kinds of fiction that had become available. The titles of two of these books promise "lives" and at least one implies that the story is true. The same promise appears on the title page of *Moll Flanders:* "The Fortunes and Misfortunes of the Famous Moll Flanders, &c. Who was Born in Newgate, and during a Life of continu'd Variety for Three-score Years . . . Written from her own Memorandums." Until well into the eighteenth century, most fiction claimed to be true and appeared with a first-person narrator.

Such claims made these books more appealing. In the first place, they asserted that they were not "lies," and enough of the puritan spirit lingered to make fiction and time spent reading fiction suspect. Second, they seemed to promise education through experience. Most of the literature of the period had, or purported to have, a didactic purpose, and the narrators' offers of their experience for the benefit of readers reminded readers of the adage "experience is the best teacher." After all, history and sermon exempla operated through instructive anecdotes and lives. Defoe is careful to make these claims for his book. Deliberately setting *Moll Flanders* apart from the forms then recognized as fictional if not downright fantastic, Defoe begins the preface, "The World is so taken up of late with Novels and Romances, that it will be hard for a private History to be taken for Genuine." It continues with his claim of the book's usefulness: "this Book is recommended to the Reader, as a Work from every part of which something may be learned, and some just and religious Inference is drawn, by which the Reader will have something of Instruction."[2]

Written on an engrossing, topical subject, *Moll Flanders* captured a fascinating part of London life, made all the respectable contemporary claims for fiction, and continues to entertain its readers today.

CHAPTER 2

The Importance of the Work

Very few books in the history of any nation hold both literary and popular appeal; *Moll Flanders* is one of these books. It has come to be one of the most popular of all eighteenth-century novels and the most widely read novel by Defoe. Not even *Robinson Crusoe* can compete with its sales. The book's resilient, optimistic heroine with her myriad adventures, griefs, and escapes and the story's happy ending appeal to all kinds of readers. The richly detailed world Defoe creates gives the novel profundity and resonance. Readers can learn about the England of Defoe's time even as they must confront enduring moral, economic, and social questions. Above all, they can enjoy the underworld career of one of literature's greatest heroines.

Moll Flanders is recognized as a landmark in the history of fiction and praised for its originality in terms such as these:

> De Foe had only one predecessor. This was Chaucer .... Chaucer was the father of English poetry, so De Foe was the father of English novel-writing. (*British Quarterly Review*, October 1869)

The Importance of the Work

> The first English author to write without imitating or adapting foreign works, . . . to devise for himself an artistic form which is perhaps without precedent . . . is Daniel Defoe, father of the English novel. (James Joyce, "Daniel Defoe," 1912)

> Very few writers have created for themselves both a new subject and a new literary form to embody it. (Ian Watt, *Rise of the Novel*, 1957)

When *Moll Flanders* was published in 1722, prose fiction was in its infancy. Readers could choose among novellas (often translated and adapted from the French, Spanish, and Italian), travel narratives, spiritual autobiographies, fictional memoirs (again, often translated from Continental works), and little else. John Bunyan's *Pilgrim's Progress* (1678) was a lonely masterpiece before Defoe's own *Robinson Crusoe* (1719).

Moll Flanders helped establish many of the characteristics we most often use in describing the form we now call "novel." Among these defining qualities are its specificity of referential detail, its easy movement from the external world to the internal world of the character's mind, its contemporaneity, its focus on an individual with some psychological depth, and even its shape, which allows digressions and varying amounts of space—sometimes more, sometimes less—to incidents that might have been of equal importance and, therefore, been given equal space.

Above all, "novel" is a referential form. It creates a specific time and place that the reader can test against a known reality, and Defoe is a master of this technique. His novels are full of objects, actual places, and even real people. Part of the referential quality of novels is the creation of human experience that seems to be both credible and individual. The protagonist, if not like us, has feelings and motives that we can understand. As the work proceeds, this character becomes somewhat consistent and, therefore, predictable. Unlike other literary forms, the novel usually demands that the reader identify with the hero or heroine, that is, move inside the character's experience. Defoe manages to get his readers to understand and sympathize with a character very unlike themselves: a female criminal.

In order to achieve this kind of sympathy, Defoe makes sure that we slip smoothly back and forth from the world of early modern England and America to Moll's thoughts and reflections. Defoe describes, for example, a small shop and its occupants; Moll assesses the situation, takes her booty, and then the narrative moves into her spiraling reactions to her deed. Anthony Burgess once said that we come to the novel for characters,[1] to see "human beings in action," and *Moll Flanders* gives us that. Moll dominates the book that bears her name, and no one who reads her story ever forgets her. The little girl who stands in the center of the group of laughing women and insists that she wants to be a gentlewoman, the woman who accidentally marries her brother and lives in terror, the optimist who mistakenly marries a highwayman and sends a message to him in the wind, the thief who steals the horse and then can't figure out what to do with it, the old lady who finds herself in Newgate prison once again the center of a circle of jeering people—these are images that last. Above all, we like the Moll Flanders who picks herself up and starts over no matter what happens, who allows herself no complaints and little time for regret, and who concludes by assuring her reader that she is "in good heart and health."

The novel is the story of Moll's life, and the episodic nature of the book fits her experience; in other terms, then, form fits function. Moll knows that she wants economic and domestic security, but circumstances and accidents prevent any kind of planning. As soon as she thinks she is "set for life," someone dies or she makes a discovery that sends her on her way again. Some parts of her life have considerable narrative unity, and they correspond to times of strong emotional involvement. Moll's seduction by the older brother and her marriage to her own brother are two examples. In both cases, she has made strong attachments, and these attachments involve places and households, not just individuals.

Other parts of Moll's life seem to be composed of a series of incidents, of variations on ways to be unlucky in love or on kinds of minor thefts. Here Moll may seem to be drifting with the current. A change or an opportunity soon interrupts, however; Moll's fears or her hopes rise again and, with them, the emotional intensity of the narrative. Sometimes the narrative passes over incidents that could have been expanded, as it does with the sketchy treatment of her time in the Mint. This pattern, like the digressions and apparent irrelevancies, mimics the experience of most actual lives and contributes to the reader's sense of the reality and immediacy of *Moll Flanders*. Since Defoe, we have come to expect these characteristics in the mainstream novel.

CHAPTER 3

Critical Reception

Moll Flanders has always been one of Defoe's most popular novels. It required three editions in its first year, was reissued the next year, and was serialized in *The London Post, the freshest and most remarkable occurrences at home and abroad* between 14 May 1722 and 20 May 1723.[1] Published in the days before widespread book reviewing and by no means pretending to be anything but popular fiction, its initial reception must be measured in ways unfamiliar to modern readers. Chapbooks, abridgments, and editions with changed events and different endings—rather than sales figures and informed commentary—mark its popularity. For instance, a pirated abridgement appeared as early as 1723, and *The London Post* ended its serialization with Moll's death, burial, and final will, in which Moll's "real name" (Susan Atkins) appeared. This version, with its altered ending, survived beside Defoe's and remained popular for nearly a century. In *Imagining the Penitentiary,* John Bender quotes a contemporary as saying that Defoe's crime books were for the "better Sort" while broadsheets and dying speeches were for the rabble.[2] A contemporary slur, however, from the 1729 *Flying Post* seems to portray at least part of his readership accurately: "Down in the Kitchen, honest Dick and Doll/Are Studying Col. Jack and Flanders Moll."[3]

In fact, Defoe was probably pleased with the book's reception. At that time, he was investing in land and, in spite of his advanced age, trying to start over as a merchant. As a professional writer in need of money, the sales of the book had to please him. Such writers were often called "hacks" in his day and pejoratively contrasted to writers with patronage or private wealth. In the *Review* he gave his response to rivals who chided him about writing for money: "the *Lawyer* pleads for his Bread, the *Soldier* fights for Bread, . . . the *Players* act for Bread, and . . . the *Clergy* preach for Bread—And where is the Man does any thing . . . but for Bread, that is, Gain?"[4] The reproach, then, applies not just to himself but to all. Although no records for payment for *Moll Flanders* survive, Defoe usually got a little more money for editions after the first, and he may even have received a few guineas for the serialization. With each edition, Defoe received a number of free copies of his books. Over the years, he had made contact with booksellers in towns as scattered as Edinburgh and Norwich, and they would sell the books for him.

Because the novel championed several causes that Defoe believed in, such as the encouragement of the settlement of North America and the recently passed act to transport criminals to the colonies, Defoe was probably gratified by its reception. After years as a political pamphlet and periodical writer, he had begun to use longer, fictional forms for propaganda, and *Moll Flanders,* like his more obviously topical *The Journal of the Plague Year,* commented on government action. For these purposes, a relatively low-class readership was desirable, for they suffered from unemployment and could be useful in the colonies. All writers, however, write "to express the life that is in them," and Defoe was surely no exception. He gives himself over to Moll's rambling life, spins out her thoughts, and makes her a wonderful individual character and an effective vehicle for expressing many of his life-long opinions.

In the second half of the eighteenth century, reviewers and

critics who mentioned Defoe's "secondary novels" or his still-popular non-fiction prose works like *The Family Instructor* or *A Tour thro' the Whole Island of Great Britain* hardly ever mentioned *Moll Flanders,* but when they did it was with disapproval. George Chalmers, generally one of Defoe's admirers, spoke for many when he wrote: "I am not convinced, that the world has been made much wiser, or better, by the perusal of these lives: they may have diverted the lower orders, but I doubt if they have much improved them. . . . They do not exhibit many scenes which are welcome to cultivated minds."[5] Anecdotes bear out the power—and the dubious influence—of the book. In *Realism, Myth, and History in Defoe's Fiction* Maximillian E. Novak recounts a meeting between George Borrow, the nineteenth-century prose writer, translator, and traveler, and an old woman with a fruit stall:

[Borrow] notices that she is reading a book "intently" and then finds himself grasped by her as he leans over the edge to see a boat caught in the swift-moving waters. She has been watching him and concluded that he was a pickpocket down on his luck who decided to put an end to his life. He enters into conversation with her and discovers that she has a son at Botany Bay [Australia] as a transported felon and that she sees no harm in stealing. . . . Her views on theft are conditioned by her continued love for her thieving son who certainly would not do anything wrong and by her admiration for the heroine of the book she reads so eagerly—Moll Flanders. To the author's question about the "harm" in theft, she responds: "No harm in the world, dear! . . . would the blessed woman in the book here have written her life as she has done, and given it to the world, if there had been any harm in faking? She, too, was what they call a thief and a cutpurse; ay, and was transported for it, like my dear son; and do you think she would have told the world so, if there had been any harm in the thing? Oh, it is a comfort to me that the blessed woman was transported, and came back—for come back she did, and rich too—for it is an assurance to me that my dear son, who was transported too, will come back like her."

Borrow . . . offers to buy the book from her as soon as he discovers in it "the air, the style, the spirit" of Defoe, but she refuses to sell it. "Without my book," she tells him, "I should mope and pine, and perhaps fling myself into the river." Instead, for six pence, she allows him to read it whenever he comes by. The one time that Borrow . . . takes advantage of the chance to read, he finds himself so engrossed in it that hours pass by without his taking his eyes off the pages before him. (71–72)

Throughout the nineteenth century, *A Journal of the Plague Year,* *Memoirs of a Cavalier,* and even *Colonel Jack* received more attention and praise than *Moll Flanders.* Even a sympathetic biographer, Walter Wilson, agreed that the scenes in *Moll Flanders* "must be always unwelcome to a refined and well-cultivated mind." As late as 1916, William Trent, another biographer of Defoe, said that part of the title was unprintable ("was Twelve Year a Whore, five times a Wife [whereof once to her own Brother]").[6]

Turn-of-the-century critics, however, were beginning to praise Defoe's work for the quality still most closely associated with his novels: his verisimilitude, his ability to create "an undeviating likeness to real life," as Walter Wilson said. Sir Walter Scott had compared Defoe's ability to portray characters like Moll to "the gipsy-boys of the Spanish painter Murillo, which are so justly admired, as being, in truth of conception, and spirit of execution, the very *chef d'oeuvres* of art." Increasingly, recognition of the "other" novels followed, but writers often searched for the reasons for their inferiority to *Robinson Crusoe.* Leslie Stephen, for instance, found "one or two forcible situations" in each of the novels, but pronounced *Moll* "about as wearisome as the journal of a specially heartless lady of the same character would be at the present day." Some critics, however, pointed out these novels' similarities to *Crusoe* and the appeal of *Moll Flanders, Roxana, Colonel*

Jack, and *Captain Singleton.* One of those critics, Charles Lamb, said they bore the "veritable impress of De Foe" and pointedly asked, "But are there no solitudes out of the cave and desert?" By the end of the century, serious novel scholars, such as Wilbur Cross, the biographer of Henry Fielding, had begun to compare Defoe to the modern naturalists, or, in Alan Dugald McKillop's later terms, "the hard-boiled novelists."

In 1919, Virginia Woolf was commissioned to write an essay on Defoe to commemorate the two-hundredth anniversary of the publication of *Robinson Crusoe.* She used the opportunity to praise *Moll Flanders* and *Roxana.* "They stand," she wrote, "among the few English novels which we can call indisputably great."[7] The tide turned quickly. In an important book, *The English Novel: Form and Function,* published in 1953, Dorothy Van Ghent praised the way Defoe could make the subject of money "not sordid but tragic when it stands not for ease and consequence but for honour, honesty, and life itself." Critical commentary burgeoned after Alan Dugald McKillop's *Early Masters of English Fiction* and Ian Watt's *Rise of the Novel,* both published in the mid-fifties. On the first page of his book McKillop said, "Defoe's contribution to fiction has never been fully analyzed, interpreted, or even identified." He went on to praise the realism of *Moll Flanders* and to list some of its artistic excellencies. Watt wrote the most extended and searching essay yet devoted to *Moll Flanders* and opened avenues of critical debate that still draw comment. As Watt points out in a later article, only three articles or other discussions had appeared between 1945 and 1955.

Criticism about the novels, and *Moll Flanders* in particular, has increased exponentially since then. Like much of the criticism about Defoe's works, that of *Moll Flanders* has often been concerned with the context of the work. For instance, chapters in G. A. Starr's books relate *Moll Flanders* to spiritual autobiographies and to the popular casuistical writing of the period. Maximillian Novak's *Economics and the Fiction of Defoe* and *Defoe and the Nature of Man* were important studies of the ways

Defoe integrated political, economic, and philosophical theory into his fiction and played an important part in raising Defoe's status. In the sixties, many critics debated the question raised by Van Ghent and pursued by Watt of whether or not the book was intentionally ironic. To some extent, that matter is still debated.

The major critical works since then have tried to demonstrate that Defoe was a deliberate, conscious artist rather than a digressive, rambling writer who simply sat down and wrote copiously and carelessly. McKillop had said that Defoe's use of detail was "casual and apparently unstudied" but "always bears on the main point, even though given in a repetitious and colloquial style." Watt had called him the master of impersonation, found Moll Flanders "suspiciously like her author," and identified her narrative as written in "Defoe's usual style." Thus Defoe became a writer whose art was highly autobiographical or "natural." Rather than referring to biography or irony to explain technique and apparent contradictions in the book, later critics have pointed out clusters of images and pervading language patterns that suggest strong thematic and tonal unities. Books such as Everett Zimmerman's *Defoe and the Novel* and David Blewitt's *Defoe's Art of Fiction* consider the developing sophistication and apparently deliberate experimentation in Defoe's novels and set *Moll Flanders* in this kind of progression. By the mid-seventies, a few critics, notably Paul Alkon and John Richetti, had published book-length, theoretically ambitious studies, and Defoe criticism had come of age.

In the last few years, studies of *Moll Flanders* have delineated its cultural contexts and integrated theoretical studies of popular literature; among these are Ian Bell's *Defoe's Fiction* and my *Daniel Defoe: Ambition and Innovation* and *Daniel Defoe: His Life*. It is clear that *Moll Flanders,* like all popular fiction, has formulaic elements and allows readers to indulge their fantasies (some illicit), but in the conclusion it reaffirms the mores of the majority culture. Ian Bell points out that the best of this fiction promises that the narrative form is familiar, even conventional, but also that it is somehow special. He sees *Moll Flanders* as a combination of the criminal tale, the female adventure, and the repentance story and finds its originality in the "handling of psychological notions like guilt and misery" (149). *Defoe: Ambition and Innovation* focuses on readers' desire for vicarious experience and knowledge and on "the appeal of the confrontation between ordinary, unheroic individuals and the unknown" as they struggle to fulfill a rags-to-riches fantasy. These books place *Moll Flanders* in the context of popular literature, and, by doing so, clarify Defoe's originality and his contribution to the development of the literary form we call "novel."

Moll Flanders continues to attract considerable critical attention. Debate about the book has always centered on its ethical stance. This search for a coherent moral structure that will explain Defoe's own opinion or moral position is consistent with an emphasis prevalent in English and American novel criticism since its inception, a tendency to lay stress on moral seriousness that was strengthened by Matthew Arnold and especially F. R. Leavis. The contradiction between Moll's often reprehensible actions and her delightful character has led scholars to condemn Defoe's own morality, to debate the degree of irony in his presentation and especially in the narrative voice, and to argue that the novel captures the ambiguity of the actual world. Explanations and contributions to existing controversies on this point continue to be published.

The movement of literary criticism in recent years has been toward regarding the work as a text, a product of culture that has nearly infinite relationships; thus criticism now places works in ever richer and more diverse contexts. This trend has added to the interest in the novel. For instance, application of the theories of Michel Foucault, Jonathan Culler, Mikhail Bakhtin, and others has enriched our understanding of the cultural meanings in the novel and highlighted the paradigms of organization inscribed in the novel. For instance, John Richetti in *Defoe's Narratives* shows how Moll's efforts to discover a coherent self illuminate the struggle of the self with restricting social and ideological realities; John Bender in *Imagining the Penitentiary* argues that books such as *Moll Flanders* are "vehicles, not the reflections, of social change" and participate in the evolution of social institutions such as the penitentiary.

Although the titles of *Robinson Crusoe* and *Journal of the Plague Year* may be more familiar to ordinary people and have better artistic reputations, *Moll Flanders* is the Defoe novel most frequently taught in colleges and universities. The rising number of fine Marxist critics, the popularity of social history, and the rise of the new historicism have contributed to the novel's reputation as a book rich in ideas. The unforgettable heroine, her uncrushable spirit, and her adventures, mishaps, and disasters continue to give enjoyment to all kinds of readers. Because of its popular appeal and literary quality, because critics since Watt have agreed that it is more typical of the mainstream English and American novel than *Robinson Crusoe,* and because it may address questions of more interest to a secular age and to female students who increasingly outnumber male literature students, *Moll* appears on the reading lists for freshmen through graduate courses. Above all, readers find life in it. As William Faulkner once said, "When I remember Moll Flanders and all her teeming and rich fecundity like a marketplace where all that had survived up to that time must bide and pass [I can wish I had written that book]."[8]

A Reading

CHAPTER 4

Story and Structure

Since the beginning of time, people have loved stories. The earliest records of civilization include hints of them. One of the most basic patterns stories have is a series of adventures undertaken or experienced by a single hero. These adventures may be "tall tales," clever tricks, or struggles with the hardships of life. In the early romances, the hero had to battle both natural and supernatural foes and some sort of quest was built into the story. *Moll Flanders* has much in common with this beloved pattern, and Defoe has given us a heroine rather than a hero. By doing so, he has intensified the struggle; without a man's strength, education, social advantages, and expectations, Moll's dreams of a secure middle-class life are castles in the air, for she soon has to combat starvation.

From the very beginning of the book, Defoe holds our interest. The preface, written by a fictional "editor," explains that we will read the life of a shocking woman criminal, one whose language is too scandalous for print. As this narrator says, "When a Woman debauch'd from her Youth, nay, even being the Offspring of Debauchery and Vice, comes to give an Account of all her vicious Practises, and even to descend to the particular Occasions and Circumstances by which she first became wicked, and of all the progressions of Crime which she run through in threescore Year, an Author must be hard put to it to wrap it up . . . clean"(1). The beginning of her story reinforces the idea of her evil life, for she tells us that her name is so well-known in the records of the court and the prison that even now, in her repentant old age, she cannot tell us her true name.

By the third page, she has told us she was the daughter (probably illegitimate) of a transported felon, had been carried around by a band of gypsies, and finally turned over to one of the women who kept charity children for a parish in Colchester, Essex. Such children were fed and clothed from the "poor tax" (a small sum levied against all of those who owned houses or a certain amount of property) and donations from sympathetic citizens. Most of them were "put to service" by age seven, sent out to be servants on farms or in households. That is what Moll's future is supposed to be. Almost immediately Moll's strong aversion to being a servant and her love for cleanliness, good manners, and neat, respectable dress emerge, and the conflict begins between what society expects and what she hopes. Defoe emphasizes the contrast between Moll's dreams and her actual possibilities throughout this early section, begins to prepare us for Moll's prolonged maneuverings to avoid things that seem to be her inevitable fate, and establishes her personality as one that either cannot or will not see herself as others see her.

The "nurse" with whom Moll has been placed allows her to stay longer than most children. Soon, however, the woman dies, and Moll is taken into the house of one of the women who has petted her and enjoyed her pretensions. Although it appears that she has gone from one loving, protective environment to another, this is not so, and the book begins in earnest. The novel as a whole is straightforward and breaks into three parts. The first part describes Moll's childhood and first love affair; the second traces her attempts to find domestic and economic security through marriage; and the third recounts her career as a thief.

Story refers to the events arranged in chronological order and is usually distinguished from "plot," which demands that the reader interpret the action. Readers look for relationships and attempt to assign causality. Another great novelist, E. M. Forster, in *Aspects of the Novel,* gave these two helpful examples:

Story: "The king died and the queen died."
Plot: "The queen died, no one knew why, until it was discovered that it was through grief at the death of the king." (60)

When readers "plot" the story, they see how Defoe has selected episodes to narrate and has assigned causes and motives for events. By making these relationships, they can begin to surmise or even to identify and interpret some of Defoe's ideas about the world and human nature. In order to help readers interpret, authors build patterns into their books. Some of these patterns, including the one with its hero and his series of adventures, have come to tell readers what to expect. Such narratives give many pleasures, such as the recognition of the pattern, the predictability of the increasingly ingenious conflicts, and the security of knowing that the protagonist will triumph. In order to hold readers' interest, writers add original or even startling touches such as fantastic monsters, exotic settings—or a heroine. Special significance may be signalled by such departures from the norm.

As might be expected from Defoe's use of the romance pattern, *Moll Flanders* seems quite episodic. In fact, one scholar has counted more than one hundred individual incidents. Defoe used two other familiar narrative structures, both of which happen to include numerous adventures, and all three are highly linear. One of these structures, the spiritual autobiography, recounted the crimes and degeneration of the individual and then described how salvation came about; the other, the criminal lives, described the corruption, criminal careers, and punishments of malefactors. Especially for unsophisticated readers, such patterns provide guideposts for understanding and interpretation. Defoe also uses incremental repetition as well as any twentieth-century advertiser to emphasize the lessons he wants his readers to learn. From the very first pages when he has Moll Flanders remark that she has heard that, in neighboring countries, the government takes responsibility for orphans and assures that they learn a trade, Defoe expresses his own opinions pointedly, and he repeats the most important ones several times in several different ways.

Rhythm and pattern, whether in music, the seasons, or in a story, give us pleasure. As Forster said, "Whereas the story appeals to our curiosity and the plot to our intelligence, the pattern appeals to our aesthetic sense."[1] *Moll Flanders* begins with Moll's birth and ends with her prosperous old age. Within this time-span, each part begins dramatically and proceeds as swiftly as the first section. From the point in the story that begins when the older brother grabs and kisses her (21–22) to the time when she is forced to marry his brother, the book has many rhythmic similarities to the other sections even as it functions as foundation. Each encounter with the older brother is an episode; the incidents have a progressive nature and an inexorable movement that determines that the reader will both dread and expect the outcome. When the older brother's kiss and flattering words "fire her blood," the reader knows she is lost. The end of that affair is as inevitable as the day Moll becomes too old for the marriage market and the day her crimes lead to her arrest.

The second part of the book begins after her first husband, the younger brother, Robin, dies. They had lived in London and Moll sees the city as a marriage market and intends to use her inherited money and physical attractiveness to bargain her way into a good marriage. She is a different character now, and the hardening process common to criminal lives and spiritual autobiography is already evident. This pattern of the book is strongly linear. She had believed the older brother, had held the romantic hopes typical of a young girl, and had argued for unrealistic, even fantastic plans with him. In London, she says, "I had been trick'd once by *that Cheat call'd LOVE,* but the Game was over; I was resolv'd now to be Married, or Nothing, and to be well Married, or not at all" (60). Things that she had overheard in Colchester are now part of her view of the world; for instance, in discussing her once, the family had agreed: "*Betty* wants but one Thing, but she had as good want every Thing . . . if a young Woman have Beauty, Birth, Breeding, Wit, Sense, Manners, Modesty, and all these to an Extream; yet if she have not Money, she's no Body, she had as good want them all" (20). At that time, Moll had denied her low status just as she had not really understood the implications of their words.

In her pursuit of a husband, she resorts to tricks and to increasingly serious deceptions. She goes to Bath and says coldly, "The Bath is a place of gallantry enough; expensive, and full of snares; I went thither indeed in the view of taking what might offer." In her youth, she had been ensnared; now she freely describes herself as a snare. She lives with a married man she meets there, then bears his child, and, when he repents, tricks him out of a last £50. Soon after, she keeps an honest bank clerk (who has divorced his wife for her) dangling while she bears yet another man's child.

Each transition in the novel is marked by times when Moll experiences anxiety that approaches panic. She feels both destitute and desperate. Defoe, as he had in several nonfiction works, demands that the reader recognize what the results of this state of mind may be. Moll says, "But there are Temptations which it is not in the Power of Human Nature to resist, and few know what would be their Case, if driven to the same Exigences" (188). As the older brother makes clear that his sexual interest in Moll is at an end, that he will allow her to be turned out, and that she could end up "a meer cast-off whore" without either brother, she describes herself as terrified, trapped, and desperate.

The last part begins as dramatically as the others. After the bank clerk dies, she finds herself too old and too poor to compete in the marriage market and lives two years in anxiety and indecision. Her state of mind is close to that before she married Robin. She describes herself as in "dismal Circumstances, and as it were only bleeding to Death, without the least hope or prospect of help from God or Man; . . . and I began to be Desperate, for I grew Poor apace" (190). One day she impetuously steals a bundle that a careless maid has set down. She says, "It is impossible to express the Horror of my Soul," but almost immediately she walks the streets "I knew not whither, and in search of I knew not what" (192–194). In fact, she is waiting for an opportunity for another theft. She meets a child who has been at dancing school, takes the child's gold necklace, and even thinks of "killing the child in the dark alley." The pattern of hardening becomes unmistakable. After this theft, many more follow; Moll steals from struggling shopkeepers and from people whose homes are burning down; she even extorts a dinner from one of her victims. She says of herself, "I was enter'd a compleat Thief, harden'd to a Pitch above all the Reflections of Conscience or Modesty" (202). She can describe hearing that one of her associates has been hanged as "joyful news . . . the best news . . . that I had heard a great while."

The pattern of Moll's hardening dramatizes the dreadful degeneration of a child who develops the worst kind of criminal mind. As G. A. Starr has said, Moll's "pretense of necessity gives way to frank avarice."[2] This progress is accompanied by the reader's constant awareness of what must be Moll's inevitable destiny: Newgate Prison. In fact, the number of times Moll mentions it and the ways Defoe has her react to it give the novel an element of suspense. Newgate seems to loom larger and larger; each of Moll's crimes and her increasingly narrow escapes promise her capture. Moll knows that she was born there, and when she is put in Newgate she describes it as "the Place that had so long expected me, and which with so much Art and Success I had so long avoided" (273). Earlier she had been unable to visit her friends there, because the place affected her so deeply. To her, the prison is both hellish and a gateway to hell. It confirms what she has feared, not just about the risks she has run, but also about herself. Newgate functions as Moll's destiny, as place of punishment, and as turning point.

The novel does not end in Newgate or at Tyburn, the place where criminals were hanged in batches. As Lincoln Faller has demonstrated, most criminal biographies ended with the death of the subject.[3] Moll, however, receives a visit from a young priest and he "breaks into her soul." Moll has previously described herself as "degenerated into stone," possessed by "a strange lethargy of soul," and despairing. Because of his example and exhortations, she repents, and he is able to arrange the commuting of her sentence from hanging to transportation. Modern readers have often felt Moll's repentance unsatisfactory, and John Bender may have resolved these feelings as well as anyone by pointing out that Moll is certainly "rehabilitated" if not repentant.[4] Eighteenth-century readers probably did not share our skepticism. They would have recognized the pattern of the spiritual autobiography (a pattern codified in hundreds of religious books) in the steps to repentance that Moll goes through and would have seen Defoe's treatment as schematic rather than inadequate. She and Jemy both thank God sincerely, and Jemy's insistence that "mercies touch the heart" conforms to Defoe's often-stated opinion that tranquil rather than catastrophic times provide the best setting for serious thoughts about God. Although Lincoln Faller is interpreting the dynamics of brief criminal lives such as those by the Newgate ordinary, his work suits the dynamics of *Moll Flanders* well. Her confession and the end of her story, like those of the common criminals, serve to reunite her with the community and its mores; her repentance associates her with the saints invoked in the spiritual autobiographies.

This final scene of repentance and prosperity intersects with another structural pattern in the novel. This second pattern depends upon periodic repetitions designed to reinforce some of the major ideas. For instance, Defoe points out the significance of money and the destructive materialism of society in many ways, and Moll's careful taking stock after each adventure is one. She emerges from her first marriage with £1,200 and two children (whom her mother-in-law keeps); from her second with £500; from her marriage to her brother with £200 to £300 and two living children (whom she leaves with him), and so on. She continues her accounting throughout her criminal career. At one point she has saved £700 and "goods," a considerable fortune in the 1670s when the novel is set. When she embarks for America she takes £246, Jemy takes £108, and she leaves £300 in England. This pattern deepens the mercenary character of the book and provides a gauge not only to Moll's situation but to what she has to use to "set up" in a new life. As avarice replaces need, it indicates her hardening.

Yet another pattern of repetition depends on the kind of ironic word play Defoe enjoyed. Moll felt that her marriage to Robin was incest because of her affair and continued fantasies about the older brother. When she accidentally marries her real brother, the contrast between real incest and her first marriage makes a point that Defoe emphasized in *Robinson Crusoe*: that people are often ungrateful and don't know when they are well off. Crusoe had felt imprisoned and miserable on his Brazilian tobacco plantation; soon he is truly imprisoned on the island, and one of the things he misses most is tobacco. *Moll Flanders,* however, is closer to comedy than any other mode, and in it such ironies are not always punitive. Jemy, Moll's highwayman husband, had believed that she brought him a fortune; when they are reunited in Newgate and transported to Virginia, she does. Her money gets them to Virginia in comfort, makes them prosperous there, and is augmented by the fortune from her incestuous marriage.

Some of Defoe's purposes are rather obvious and more significant to the novel. He intends, for instance, to show the futility, even destructiveness, of imprisonment. Incremental repetitions emphasize ideas like these, which Defoe wants his readers to remember. For instance, several characters insist that Newgate makes more criminals than "all the Clubs and Societies of Villains in the Nation" (87) and, thus, argues for the benefits of transportation. Moll's mother tells her so when they talk in Virginia, and Moll's own experience in Newgate confirms the destructive effects. It is there that she sees people who are even more despairing and dissolute than those she met in the Mint. She describes the "hellish noise, the roaring, swearing and clamour, the stench and nastiness," and how the prisoners soon become apathetic, brutish, thoughtless, and coarse beyond imagination. Even she degenerates, as she says, "into stone" and comes to understand how they can sing ditties about being hanged. The central image of this pattern of repetition is the colony of Virginia rather than Newgate Prison. It is here that Moll's third husband (and fourth lover) takes her when they discover neither has the fortune the other expected. For a while, they live there in prosperity and happiness. Moll says, "I thought myself the happiest creature alive" (85).

The opposite side of this prison theme is the depiction of the benefits of transportation. Moll's mother was transported for the theft of three pieces of cloth, and Moll will be transported for a nearly identical offense. The mother married well and became a prosperous property owner. Her mother tells her all about her neighbors and explains that many had been transported as criminals or brought over to be servants. "Hence, Child," she says, "many a *Newgate* Bird becomes a great Man, and we have . . . several Justices of the Peace, Officers of the Train Bands, and Magistrates of the Towns they live in, that have been burnt in the Hand." "Justice Ba--r was a Shoplifter," she gossips (86–87). Soon she confides that she herself was branded and transported, behaved modestly, married her master, and now offers her successful life as yet another example of the benefits of transportation to the colonies.

Moll was born in Newgate, and she will be redeemed there, thus, born again upon her release to the colonies. After Moll's arrest and conviction she persuades her former husband, the highwayman Jemy, to accept transportation and go to Virginia with her. They pay for their passage (as was allowed throughout the

Restoration and eighteenth century), arrange for the purchase of their freedom, and soon find themselves rich and secure. Once again, immigration to the colonies has proved beneficial. Significantly, it is not until they settle in Virginia that Jemy and Moll feel truly thankful to God.

Defoe's nonfiction writing makes clear that he believed Great Britain's future power and prosperity depended on its colonies, and, therefore, the North American colonies needed to be populated. He laid out what we would call a vigorous imperial policy, and his books, such as *A Plan of the English Commerce* (1728), argued for encouraging existing settlements and for developing new ones. England suffered from rampant unemployment as well as crime, and both problems might be diminished by immigration. Another of Defoe's novels, *Colonel Jack,* shows a young man kidnapped and sold into servitude in Maryland, then becoming an educated, wealthy man. Together, the two novels are powerful propaganda for the colonies. The fact that contemporaries described "Dick and Doll" reading the novel "in the Kitchen" suggests that he reached the audience he hoped to persuade.

Closely related to this purpose is the way *Moll Flanders* functions as support for the Transportation Act of 1718. Defoe had been employed by the government almost all of his adult life, and soon after the accession of George I, his connection to it had been affirmed. Defoe may have seen support of the act as part of his support for the government, or he may have acted from conviction alone when he depicted transportation favorably. For the purposes of this book, it does not really matter greatly if it was one or the other or some combination. By contrasting the effects of transportation so starkly with those of imprisonment, he makes a persuasive case.

Yet another part of the book is its rhythmical narration of major events, a pattern that came to be characteristic of the novel. The external situation will be described in great detail and its impact on the protagonist made clear; the character will react; at some point, the character will contemplate the action taken. One of the most distinctive elements of *Moll Flanders* is the way she broods, analyzes, and rationalizes. Her situation and her action give way to extended thought, and the book moves smoothly from moments of rapid action to pages of intense thought. Defoe devotes a page and a half to describing her state of mind, two paragraphs to the theft of the bundle, and nearly two pages to her reactions to this first theft. Similarly, he gives a page to Moll at Bartholomew Fair and her meeting with the inebriated gentleman, a paragraph to their adultery, a paragraph to her searching "him to a nicety" and escaping, and two and a half pages to her reflections, which begin, "This was an adventure indeed unlook'd for" and go on to a lecture on the dangers of drunken sexual encounters.

This method is but one part of the easy movement between the description of Moll's physical world and her thoughts. She seems to enjoy describing exactly how she made arrangements, ensnared husbands, and outwitted robbery victims, and she itemizes her emotions with the same attention she gives to listing her profits. Readers can follow her thoughts as precisely as they can map her movements through the city streets. They come to trust the fullness as well as the variety of her tale and give themselves over to her consciousness.

CHAPTER 5

Setting

The setting, where the author locates the book's action, helps design the world in which the character lives. Most of *Moll Flanders* takes place in the City of London, the one square mile part of what was then the largest metropolitan area in Europe. The Old City, as it is often called today, is a maze of winding, narrow streets that suddenly open before mighty buildings: St. Paul's Cathedral, the Guildhall, the Bank of England. Defoe loved this part of London; he mentions dozens of its coffeehouses in his essays and letters, recounts amusing anecdotes collected on its streets, and returns to die there at age seventy-one. Because the buildings are numerous and close together and the streets so narrow, this part of London can be dark and even claustrophobic. Just as often, however, the Old City reveals delightful surprises. An archway reveals a tiny, lovely garden like the Draper's court that was close to one of Defoe's childhood homes. A view down a street will suddenly frame St. Paul's, just as its architect, Christopher Wren, planned. The bright colors of one of the Livery Company banners will billow above an ornate wooden door, and the passerby will know that inside are centuries-old silver, glass, portraits, and carved furniture, including the special oversized arm chair for the Company's Master.

Moll Flanders begins in Essex, a southeastern county of rich farmland, and the novel's last detailed picture of Moll is in the fertile Virginia colony, but it is the first great novel of the city of London. Defoe loved London, and his extended description of it in his *Tour thro' the Whole Island of Great Britain* begins, "As I am now near the centre of this work, so I am to describe the great centre of England, the city of London."[1] The city colors every aspect of the novel and captures the feel of all modern cities as surely as it describes the London where Defoe lived.

Moll moves through its parishes and streets; she blends anonymously with the fashionable in St. James Park, with the crowds of shoppers in the Strand, with the fugitives in the Mint; and she slips into Clerkenwell to sell her booty. Street names and Old City landmarks roll off her tongue, and she seems equally at home at Leadenhall market, on the Mall, at the St. Catherine's docks, at the elegant Spring Garden near Chelsea, and at a Covent Garden gambling house. Yet the very anonymity that the city gives her emphasizes the loneliness, alienation, and individuality that are so important to Defoe's themes. She comes to London the first time with one of the bitterest lessons life can teach a young girl, a lump still in her throat: she says, "I had been trick'd once by *that Cheat call'd LOVE*." Shortly afterwards, she writes, "Money's Vertue; Gold is Fate" (79). Time after time she dresses to blend in with a particular group of people found in the streets, yet nearly as often Defoe shows her pausing and feeling alone, singular, and herself. For instance, in the midst of a crowd she comments, "I had very good Cloths on, and a Gold Watch by my Side, as like a Lady as other Folks" (211). She sits alone and has a pint of ale in a pub, walks the streets alone, and even attends Bartholomew Fair by herself.

The modern city forces an awareness of essential solitariness that no other setting does. Although a person standing alone by the sea can feel dwarfed by nature and its forces, and one sitting alone on a hillside contemplating a vast plain can feel singular, both can take false comfort in the fact that they can retrace their steps and rejoin people in a home, a coffee shop, a store, or on a busy street. The city dweller confronts the lie buried in this illusion. On the busiest street, at the liveliest eating establishment, this person can suddenly feel as isolated as the farthest star. As Defoe had Robinson Crusoe point out in "Of Solitude" in the *Serious Reflections of Robinson Crusoe*, "life in general is . . . but one universal act of solitude" and "man may be properly said to be alone in the midst of the crowds and hurry of men and business." He could even experience "much more solitude in the middle of the greatest collection of mankind in the world, I mean London," he continued, meaning, perhaps, that in the city he might feel truly alone while on the island he had always felt the presence of God.[2] Moreover, the city's numerous buildings with their closed doors and secret purposes symbolize closed opportunities as country roads and rail fences never do. It takes an effort of will and resilient optimism to see a cityscape as opportunity day after day.

Yet the city has always represented a new start, and the anonymity it offers seems to allow the remaking of the personality and reputation as well as of the fortune. When Moll and Robin move there, Moll can hold at bay the memories of the older brother, her seduction, and the disappointed in-laws. When Robin dies, the city seems a marriage-market to Moll and, thus, a chance for a happier life. Her hopes are bright as she seeks a prosperous man of "mirth and wit." She is optimistic, for she "put no small value" upon herself and joins a circle of friends with a woman who was "one of the maddest, gayest things alive." Soon, however, she finds the liveliest men had no interest in marriage and the woman "not so much Mistress of her Vertue" as she should have been. In an attempt to unite her desire for pleasure and her need for security, she marries a "gentleman-tradesman," a draper who spends her money—much of it on her—and then leaves her to flee to the Mint, the part of London where debtors had legal sanctuary.

From this point on, the commercial nature of the city dominates. Moll increasingly talks of herself as a commodity and bargains, barters, and cheats her way through life. Much has been written about this capitalistic language, and a glance at the episode of her third marriage serves as sufficient example. She moves with a friend out of the Mint and embarks on her next quest for a husband with these words:

> This Knowledge I soon learnt by Experience, (*viz.*) That the State of things was altered, as to Matrimony, and . . . that Marriages were here the Consequences of politick Schemes, for forming Interests, and carrying on Business, and that LOVE had no Share, or but very little in the Matter.
> That, as my Sister in Law at *Colchester* had said . . . Money only made a Woman agreeable. . . .
> . . . as the Market run very Unhappily on the Men's side, I found the Women had lost the Privilege of saying No. (67)

She describes the men as openly, unapologetically going "a Fortune Hunting, as they call it" and herself as "setting up" to get a husband, the words habitually used to mean stocking and opening a shop. With her friend's help she moves, dresses carefully, and, like a Venus flytrap, waits for the right victim. Words like "cheap," "bargain," and "stock" reoccur, and later she compares herself to "a bag of money."

Patricia Meyer Spacks has pointed out that, as well as being a marriage market, the city encourages female dreams of self-determination and provides women characters "temporary means of assertion."[3] Moll exhibits those ambitions. She believes she can choose a husband and is far from passive once a desirable prospect comes in sight. The death of her banker husband, however, forces her to test the possibilities. Her career as a thief is an extreme example of independent self-assertion and provides her with the first true economic independence of her life. She often speaks of her crimes as her trade and considers her time learning as an apprenticeship. She sometimes calls her booty her "purchases," and her fear of apprehension may have been little more severe than the anxiety London shopkeepers and investors felt about bankruptcy.

The City provides a perfect setting for the predatory world in which Defoe places Moll. Although she was no less commodity and victim in Colchester, the city makes her condition obvious. No matter what despicable act she commits, Defoe provides a mirror. She might be looking at herself when she spars with the Virginia planter or when she and Jemy talk. Locked in a courtship ritual that includes as predominant thrust the ferreting out of economic information and the concern with self-preservation, each person is alike. Surely one of the most striking moments in the book occurs when Moll has gone to the house fire to steal and encounters a woman there for the same purpose. For a moment they stare into each other's eyes and recognize themselves. Beneath every act self-interest lurks, and bonds are forged by mutual needs. In an especially dehumanizing scene, Defoe shows pregnant women—like Moll—paying Mother Midnight to dispose of the "products" of their bodies, their babies. So many are there that some must be boarded with other women. In a gruesome twist, Mother Midnight profits from their labor, because their society has ceased to value its produce.

Once Moll has become a thief, the streets express her moods. The winding, indirect route from Leadenhall Street where she has stolen the bundle to Thames Street where she stops to rest expresses her panic, confusion, and fear, but it also symbolizes the path that has led her to her present predicament. When she steals the child's necklace, she takes an equally twisted overlong route to get from Bartholomew Close to Holborn Bridge, and her horror at having contemplated murder suggests the danger of her twisted thoughts. Later, protean in costume and demeanor, she blends into any crowd in appearance and mood as long as she can stay within certain boundaries of dress. Believing herself to be neat and genteel, she succeeds but awkwardly and uneasily in dirty rags and in men's clothing. The streets she frequents in these disguises are correspondingly ugly, as are the Clerkenwell coach stop on St. John's Street and the warehouses along the Thames near the Tower of London. It is when she is dressed as a beggar that she steals the horse and meets the worst criminals, including counterfeiters and a gang of housebreakers. Dressed as a gentlewoman, often with gloves, gold watch, hat, and veil, she goes to the parks, Foster Lane, and the fashionable shops. In these places, she chats easily with people, laments the frequency of watch snatchings, enjoys the sights as well as the opportunities, and even makes jokes.

The modern city as place of opportunity, isolation, self-assertion, freedom, and indifference evokes feelings well expressed by the modern poet Adrienne Rich, who describes her relationship to New York as "love":

> The city as object of love, a love not unmixed with horror and anger, the city as Baudelaire and Rilke had previsioned it, or William Blake for that matter, death in life, but a death emblematic of the death that is epidemic in modern society, and a life more edged, more costly, more charged with knowledge, than life elsewhere. Love as one knows it sometimes with a person with whom one is locked in struggle, energy draining but also energy replenishing, as when one is fighting for life, in oneself or someone else. Here was this damaged, self-destructive organism, preying and preyed upon. The streets were rich with human possibility and vicious with human denial.[4]

London is all of these things to Moll. She sees death and violence almost every day. Young thieves are chased by mobs, pummeled, and "pumped," repeatedly dunked in horse troughs. People throw rocks and dirt at the mercer who has accused Moll of theft and been outwitted. The rabble catch a thieving widow, and Moll describes them "dragging the poor creature in a most butcherly manner" to the shop owner. The women, and Moll herself, cannot give too much thought to the fates of the babies they hand over to Mother Midnight. Hangings are frequent. Innocence is impossible. Yet Moll feels at home there as nowhere else, learns London's ways, prospers, and returns to it as her last act.

Twice Moll tries to go "home." Once on a rambling trip, she fears arrest for her latest crime and goes to Colchester. "It was no little Pleasure that I saw the Town, where I had so many pleasant Days, and I made many Enquiries after the good old Friends, I had once had there, but could make little out, they were all dead or remov'd" (267). "Gone to London" and "all dead" echo in the paragraph and, after three or four days, Moll returns to London. Years later when she persuades Jemy to accept transportation, some of the same enthusiasm colors her dialogue and, once there, she seeks out her family. In spite of her prosperous life, her contentment with Jemy, and reunion with her son, she returns to England at the end. Another Defoe character, Colonel Jack, had compared life in the colonies to being buried alive; he says, "I could see nothing at all, and hear but a little of what was seen, and that little not till at least half a Year after it was done, and sometimes a Year or more ... this was not yet the Life of a Gentleman."[5] It is impossible to imagine Moll contentedly sitting by her fire telling tales as her own mother had. She is London, its child and its symbol.

The novel became a city form. As John Bender wrote in *Imagining the Penitentiary*, "Compilation, investigation, justification, adjudication, letters, lists, receipts, journals, records, evidentiary detail, testimony—the written traces of merchandise and manners—here is the stuff both of cities and of novels" (58). And the novel transferred the struggle for existence and the final test of strength and character from the wilderness to city streets. The beasts and barbarians of the romances became thugs, cheats, and sharpers. Already London was the ultimate test. Hundreds streamed into the city every year, and scores of them crept, destitute and bewildered, back to the provinces. Others became mindless drudges, succumbed to gin and vice, became prostitutes or thieves, or died of tuberculosis, pneumonia, or starvation. Moll pits herself against the city, nearly loses her soul, and concludes her tale, "And now notwithstanding all the Fatigues and all the Miseries [Jemy and I] have both gone thro', we are both in good Heart and Health" (342).

CHAPTER
6

Moll,
the
Criminal

Moll Flanders is remembered more for her criminal career than for her marital adventures. The numbers, occupations, and demises of the "husbands" tend to collapse, but the series of adventures, close escapes, and arrival in Newgate endure. For one thing, many of Moll's thefts are surprising; some approach the loathsome and some the comic. For another, her reactions to them are instantaneous and strong, then rapidly pushed aside. Each incident, thus, becomes immediate and distinctly rendered.

Moll, the criminal, comes from well-established lineage. From Medieval times, English people enjoyed rogue tales and "cony catcher" books. They offered the reader catalogues of crimes and ingenious tricks and created clever heroes who outwitted a series of vain, pompous, dishonest, and wealthy people. Richard Head's and Francis Kirkman's *The English Rogue* (1665, 1668, 1671) is one of the most famous of these books, and some of them, like *Long Meg of Westminster* (1635), had female protagonists. In fact, a 1573 character, the widow Edith, tricks a number of men into marrying her, usually by promising them "great abundance of gooddes," and goes on to cheat shop and inn keepers.[1]

Part of the subtitle of *The English Rogue* reads "a Complete History of the Most Eminent Cheats of Both Sexes." When Moll Flanders adeptly slips a watch off a gentlewoman's chain or talks her way out of an arrest and into a fine dinner, she is carrying on this tradition.

Of course Moll is also sister to the women tried at the Old Bailey and featured in the *Old Bailey Sessions Papers, The Ordinary of Newgate, His Account,* and the daily papers. Most of the papers carried three- or four-line items on notable crimes, arrests, trials, sentences, and hangings. By 1726 *The Post Boy,* the *London Journal,* and other papers often reported entire Old Bailey sessions, the regular days during which the judges sat in the court for serious crimes committed in London and the county of Middlesex. Reading a few months of such newspapers reveals how similar Moll was to these real women. Each Old Bailey session might try thirty to forty cases, and by 1718 booksellers made available volumes such as *A Compleat Collection of Remarkable Tryals of the Most Notorious Malefactors . . . at the Old Bailey.* Enterprising publishers such as Elizabeth Mallett printed single-page accounts or broadsides of the most interesting trials and the longer *Proceedings on the King's Commission of the Peace And Oyer and Terminer and Goal-Delivery* [sic] *of Newgate, held for the* CITY *of London, and* COUNTY *of Middlesex, at Justice-Hall in the Old Bailey.* This kind of publication was more narrative and, again, the comparisons to *Moll Flanders* are obvious. A 1703 entry reads:

Rebecca Harvey and Ann Pulham, of the Parish of St. *Dunstans* in the *West,* were indicted for privately Stealing 13 Yards of printed Callico, and 11 Yards of Muslin, out of the Shop of *John Browne,* on the 12th of *February* last. The Prosecutor said, That *Harvey* and another Woman came into the Shop, and cheapened some Callico, and took the opportunity to take the Goods, and gave them to *Pulham,* who waited for them at a distance off; but pursuing them, they were both taken, and the Goods were found upon *Pulham,* who denied the Fact, saying, That she met with one *Jenny Stephens,* who would give her six pence to carry them to the *Chequer-Inn* in *Holbourn,* but could not prove it; and they both being Confederates, the Jury found them Guilty.

An eight-page 1703 publication has as its title: *An Account of the Birth and Education, Life and Conversation of Mary Raby; Who was Executed at Tyburn on Wednesday the 3d of Nov 1703 for Fellony and Burglary & Particularly The Manner of her several pretended Marriages, first taking to Evil Company, her many Cheats, Robberies, Shop-liftings, Clipping, Coyning, Receiving Stolen Goods, and other strange and astonishing Actions of her Life, from the time of her Birth to her shameful Death. To which is added: Her Apprehension, Commitment to Newgate, her Examination, Condemnation, and last true Dying Speech at the Place of Execution. As also An Account of her Funeral, being buried in Mary bone Churchyard on Thursday last.* Moll's story, then, was a familiar one.

Moll is part of an amorphous underclass, many of whom committed occasional crimes or came to live by their robberies. The outline of her story, as the title above shows, follows a depressing, well-worn path. In her undistinguished childhood, her youthful love affairs, and her first crime, she is one of many. Just as the criminal lives depicted men and women losing their ability to feel regret or, in some cases, humanity, Moll becomes a hardened woman. Critics such as G. A. Starr, Everett Zimmerman, and Lincoln Faller have traced this pattern in detail when it appears in literature. When Moll is willing to deceive the bank clerk until she rids herself of another man's child, able to rob a woman whose house is burning down, and comes to "roll" and then blackmail a man she picks up at Bartholomew Fair, she has sunk to moral as well as criminal depths.

The formula for the criminal lives as displayed in the nonliterary material usually had six parts. They began with ancestry and upbringing and lingered a bit over any bad influences present in youth. Upon reading scores of them, readers are struck first by how many come from ordinary families and, second, how frequently the accounts blame bad company for the subject's first transgressions. Spiritual autobiographies like John Bunyan's *Grace Abounding to the Chief of Sinners* (1666) and his fictional *The Life and Death of Mr. Badman* (1680) find the roots of depravity in bad friendships. This part would show the simultaneous pleasure and discomfort of the young person, the triumph of enjoyment, and the gradual entrapment of the subject. The next part of the account, and the part seventeenth- and eighteenth-century commentators always believed (with regret) to be the most popular, recounted the offender's crimes. Here the kinds of criminal life differed, and readers learned if they were in for clever tricks, property crimes, serious brutalities, or a short progression leading to the shocking murder of a loved one. Thus, some books described increasing cleverness and others ascending evil.

The next part of the book noted the offender's capture and incarceration, and then followed a fairly lengthy section on the repentance (or nonrepentance). An important element here was the confession. Confession was an integral part of the path to salvation and occupied an important social place as well. William Talbot, Bishop of Oxford, for instance, called criminals' confessions "a Satisfaction they ow'd their Country." Lincoln Faller has called capture, trial, and punishment, "the orthodoxies that bind" people together.[2] Through their confessions and submission they rejoined society. The conclusions gave detailed accounts of the execution. Since imprisonment was not a penalty and almost all of the subjects of these lives were nonclergyable felons, the death penalty could be expected. At that time, some lesser felonies (such as damaging trees or poaching) allowed the offender to claim the ancient "benefit of clergy" for the first conviction only. In former times, the man had to show that he could read the "neck verse," Psalm 51. By the eighteenth century, the privilege had been extended to women, and such offenders were not being turned over to the representative of the Church for punishment but simply released.

Although repentance might save the soul, in Western society, it has been the basis for pardon in an infinitesimally small number of cases. Readers—and, of course, the hundreds of spectators who thronged to every hanging—could take comfort in the fact that repentant criminals were paying for their crimes but also joining the community of the blessed in Heaven. Thus, the offender simultaneously served as fearsome example to those who might be inclined to crime and as evidence of society's redeeming power, for its legal system had brought the criminal to justice *and* salvation. This rationalization undoubtedly made capital punishment more acceptable and allowed such people as the editor of the *Newgate Calendar* to say that their accounts were instructive to *families*. Hanging also provided neat closure to the story as transportation or release did not; the reader need not wonder if the repentances had been sincere or if the criminals went back to crime because they appeared at once before God's great bar of justice.

Moll Flanders conforms to this pattern closely. Even in the conclusion, it approximates the formula. Her sorrow and regret in Newgate, her confession to the minister, and her repentance provided satisfaction to the reader because they reinforced community mores and may have been interpreted as evidence of God's justice and grace working in the world. Although Moll criticizes the Newgate ordinary (the prison chaplain) for "extorting" confessions allegedly to incriminate others, she does confess fully to the young minister who comes later. Defoe brings Moll Flanders through the process up to the point of hanging; here he shows her rejoining society and even reunites her with a husband and one of her children.

Defoe, however, is an artist, not the author of a formula book. Moll's first theft establishes several significant patterns that make her an individual, novelistic personality. Moll is walking through London, and she is feeling desperate. Her banker husband has been dead for two years, and she describes herself as in a "dismal Condition," "weeping continually over my dismal Circumstances, and as it were only bleeding to Death, without the least hope or prospect of help" (190). She goes out for a walk, "Wandring thus about I knew not whither, I pass'd by an Apothecary's Shop in *Leadenhall-street*." And she finds "a little bundle wrapt in a white cloth" left unattended by a maid. She takes it (191). Her reaction is instantaneous: "It is impossible to express the Horror of my Soul. . . . I cross'd the Street indeed, and went down the first turning I came to . . . from thence I cross'd and turn'd thro' so many ways and turnings that I could never tell which way it was, nor where I went, I felt not the Ground I stept on" (192).

A number of things happen here that become the pattern of Moll's crimes. She is a rather passive thief, for she does not break into houses or force the weak; rather she waits for an opportunity, recognizes it immediately, and takes advantage of it. She is not completely passive, of course, because she walks the streets, wanders in and out of shops, and watches passers-by. She is already ready to act, but she does not use force or even make the opportunities. Second, Moll almost always feels fear. At first she expresses horror at what she has done and what her action may mean that she has become. She also immediately fears apprehension and comes to fear it more than the moral implications of the act, and that, too, indicates her hardening. When she can, Moll examines her booty, and Defoe establishes her individuality by introducing two other patterns of behavior. She catalogues what she has in minute detail and with a snob's awareness of value. For instance, among the items in the bundle, she finds "a Suit of Child-Bed Linnen . . . very good and almost new, the Lace very fine" (192).

The second pattern is even more individual: she imagines her victim's reaction with great fullness. After her first theft, she says, "it may be some poor Widow like me, that had pack'd up these Goods to go and sell them for a little Bread for herself and a poor Child, and are now starving and breaking their Hearts, for want of that little they would have fetch'd." After she steals the bundle from the woman whose house is on fire, she describes her: "the poor disconsolate Gentlewoman who had lost so much by the Fire besides; and who would think to be sure that she had sav'd her Plate and best things; how she wou'd be surpriz'd and afflicted when she should find that she had been deceiv'd, and should find that the Person that took her Children and her Goods had not come, as was pretended, from the Gentlewoman in next Street [*sic*]" (206–7).

The account of this first crime also includes a favorite quotation of Defoe's: "Give me not poverty lest I steal." Just as he said in some of his pamphlets on bankruptcy, he gave Moll a speech in which she asks the reader not to judge her until they have "seriously" reflected on how they would have coped in her situation, described as "a desolate state." As Defoe had written many times, she concludes that distress and desperation took all of the strength to resist away. She says, "But there are Temptations which it is not in the Power of Human Nature to resist, and few know what would be their Case, if driven to the same Exigences. As Covetousness is the Root of all Evil, so Poverty is, I believe, the worst of all Snares" (188).

The extent to which Defoe believed that necessity overcame reason and provided an extenuating circumstance has been much debated.[3] In fact, however, Moll is not starving and at several points in her life had earned money by making lace or by quilting. Ostensibly, she could have gone into service, the occupation she had scorned as a child. In his writing on the South Sea Bubble, the eighteenth-century English equivalent to the 1929 stock market crash in the United States, Defoe had called avarice "an unwearied vice," and Moll exhibits both avarice and insecurity to a degree that can only be called Hobbsian, an expression of the philosophy of Thomas Hobbes, who believed that the strongest human drives are for security and self-preservation. She says that "Poverty brought me into the Mire, so Avarice kept me in" (203). Moreover, she promises herself that she will quit as soon as she has a certain amount of money. Once she has that sum, however, she raises the figure; that reached, she raises the sum again. *Moll Flanders* is more a study of criminal minds and of the addictive nature of human beings than an examination of the effects of poverty. Col. Jack, another of Defoe's heroes, is far poorer than Moll, yet he struggles to give up crime and even returns what he has stolen to some of his victims.

Yet another element in the episode of Moll's first crime is her insistence that the Devil laid the snare and then prompted her to steal. Periodically Moll continues to blame the Devil. The modern reader, like some of Defoe's contemporaries, surely feels that Moll is making excuses for herself; other eighteenth-century readers would have said that the Devil was inside Moll, and whether they thought of "the evil within" or of "possession" they would not have imagined an actual voice or appearance. It is interesting, however, that many legal documents of that time still refer to the Devil. Lincoln Faller quotes one that reads, "The Devil entred so strong into him, that nothing would satisfie but he must kill her, and no other way but with the hammer."[4]

Criminal lives had as one purpose explaining how a person who belonged to a community could commit such acts, and when people have no other way of comprehending events, they often resort to the supernatural. Moll Flanders tends to mention the Devil when circumstances intersect in ways that encourage the crime. For instance, her desperation and the neglected bundle, she says, act "as if [the Devil] had spoke, for I remember, and shall never forget it, 'twas like a Voice spoken over my Shoulder, take the Bundle; be quick; do it this Moment" (191). The child, the necklace, and the dark alley prompt her to the next theft and the thought of murder (194). Similarly, the provision of the women who teach her to steal combined with her own dexterity are called the Devil's work (201–3). In a few other places, she casually says that the Devil put temptation in her way. It must be remembered that criminal lives are popular literature and, in Defoe's time, were already somewhat old-fashioned forms. Those who would look for Defoe's own opinion about Satan behind such clichés and folk-sayings as "the Devil made me do it" are being too clever by half. Throughout his life Defoe was alert to voices and the ways different groups of people expressed themselves, and he enjoyed imitating them. When Moll says, "the Devil is an unwearied Tempter" (26), she is speaking true to her character as a poorly educated woman born about 1613.

One of the often-stated purposes of the criminal lives was to inform citizens about how criminals acted in order to help readers avoid being victims. For instance, shopkeepers would see how they provided opportunities for theft. In this tradition, the "editor" of Moll's account writes, "All the Exploits of this Lady of Fame in her Depredations upon Mankind stand as so many warnings to honest People to beware of them, intimating to them by what Methods innocent People are drawn in, plunder'd, and robb'd, and by Consequence how to avoid them" (4). Moll herself will lecture her readers and give them tips as she does when she explains in some detail how to behave with watch-snatchers:

> had she [the woman whose watch Moll had attempted to get] with a Presence of Mind needful on such an Occasion, as soon as she felt the pull, not skream'd out as she did, but turn'd immediately round, and seiz'd the next body that was behind her, she had infallibly taken me.
>
> This is a Direction not of the kindest Sort to the Fraternity; but 'tis certainly a Key to the Clue of *a Pick-pocket's* Motions, and whoever can follow it, will as certainly catch the Thief as he will be sure to miss if he does not. (212–13)

Another paragraph in the "editor's" preface recommends the book on yet another basis: "[Moll's] application to a sober Life, and industrious Management at last in *Virginia,* with her Transported Spouse, is a Story fruitful of Instruction to all the unfortunate Creatures who are oblig'd to seek their Re-establishment abroad; whether by the Misery of Transportation, or other Disaster" (4). Defoe's novel appeared within a few years of the Transportation Act of 1718, and his book includes some propaganda for it. Transportation, the banishment of convicted felons to the British colonies for a specific number of years, had been used on a very limited scale since Elizabethan times as an alternative to capital punishment, and, by 1700, had become a fairly common form of conditional pardon. The judge could pronounce it, or the criminal could petition as Moll Flanders did for transportation. Here is typical text, written by a j.p.: "I reprieved them because it did not appear to me that either of them had committed any such offense before, or were ingaged in any society of offenders. . . . But they are lewd idle fellows, and it is fitting the country should be clear'd of them. They are strong able body'd men and may do good service either in her Majestys Plantations or army."[5] The secretary of state would then endorse the pardon, conditional upon the prisoner joining the army or accepting transportation. Until 1718, merchants or the prisoners themselves paid the passage to the New World. Because the infirm and female had little or no market value there, the indigent were hanged or simply released.[6]

Throughout the seventeenth and eighteenth centuries other "unfortunate creatures . . . oblig'd to seek their re-establishment abroad" were sent to America as servants. Between 1580 and 1650, some 80,000 people went, voluntarily or otherwise, to be servants in the North American colonies. Between 1651 and 1700, the figure rose to 90,000. Individuals and companies bought servants in England for the colonies; companies sometimes bought entire shiploads of them. Some of these servants volunteered to go to America; in effect, they contracted themselves to a merchant or a ship's captain for passage, and he would then sell them for a specified period of time. The unemployment in England and the decline of the apprenticeship system made such arrangements attractive; in fact, there is evidence that such indentures were acceptable partly because of their resemblance to apprenticeships or to the binding of young people to families as servants. Some of those sent to America were kidnapped; Defoe's character Colonel Jack is one of them. Roger Morrice, a

Dissenter whose three-volume diary is preserved in the Dr. Williams Library in London, mentions several trials in which prominent merchants were convicted of this crime. About one case tried in 1682, he writes, "two great Merchants are this Term Cast for Kidnapping, you know how many merchants use to buy young people that say they are willing to goe into forraine Plantations."[7] Other servants were purchased illegally and taken to America. Merchants inspected prisoners and bought the most promising, and ship's captains bought young people whom riverfront tavernkeepers had gotten drunk.

At the time Defoe wrote *Colonel Jack* and *Moll Flanders,* poor men and women—and boys and girls—were still contracting themselves for transportation, and people were still being tricked, kidnapped, and coerced into going to the colonies as servants. But the Transportation Act of 1718 meant that British citizens in large numbers were sentenced to exile in North America. This Act allowed courts to sentence even clergied felons to transportation to America. In the newspapers and Old Bailey Sessions papers, people could read who had been ordered transported and for what crimes, and those who didn't see the felons carried through the streets to the ships could read about that, too. One of Defoe's own papers, the *White-Hall Evening Post,* for instance, often described "above 100 Convicts" being taken from Newgate to Blackfriars. Between the passage of the Act in 1718 and 1775, the courts sent 30,000 convicts to the North American colonies, primarily to Maryland and Virginia, Moll's and Jack's destinations.

Defoe's novel, then, offered the curious a chance to see what Virginia and Maryland, the two most common destinations for white servants and criminals at this time, were like and how transportation came about. Many of Defoe's novels include what can only be called propaganda for the North and South American colonies, and *Moll Flanders* shows people grown respectable, even wealthy, in Virginia. Moll's mother, for instance, says, "many a *Newgate* Bird becomes a great Man, and we have . . . several Justices of the Peace . . . and Magistrates of the Towns they live in, that have been burnt in the Hand" (86). Recent research by historians has shown that the first group of transported people often did become leading citizens, although those who came later in general did not. It is also realistic of Defoe to have Moll's sentence changed after an informal appeal and for Jemy to agree to be transported before trial. Rather than take a chance on being hanged or dying of gaol fever before the trial, many people agreed to be transported. Other prisoners were still being kidnapped or sold by unscrupulous bailiffs or keepers.

The 1718 Act gave merchants contracts granting them £3 for each convict transported. In addition, the merchants could sell the prisoners' services at auction in the colonies where men now brought an average of £10, women £8 to £9, and craftsmen as much as £25. By 1722, the year *Moll Flanders* was published, about 60 percent of the convicted male, clergyable felons and 46 percent of the women were transported. In fact, about 70 percent of all the felons convicted at the Old Bailey were deported and only about 7.5 percent executed. Although the contract-holder protested, prisoners could still arrange their own passage to the colonies.[8] Moll Flanders' legal experience is authentically rendered.

Defoe's depiction of her life and Jack's included powerful propaganda for the recent Act. Because convicted felons had often been released with a punishment as mild as being branded on the thumb, large numbers of criminals were quickly and repeatedly released. Because there were no satisfactory penalties between branding and whipping at one extreme and hanging at the other, judges and juries often felt the inappropriateness of either, and the lighter sentences were imposed.[9] Moll's and Jack's cases were designed to show the appropriateness of transportation. Jack's crimes were just the kind committed by most of the felons sent over, but he had not been caught, tried, and sentenced. In any event, his kidnapping and sale were realistic. So frequently were people tricked, made drunk, or forced that a series of laws against kidnapping were passed in England and the colonies. Moll, although an old offender, is tried only once and for theft of goods valued at £46. To have hanged a person who was technically a first offender for that crime would have seemed cruel even to an eighteenth-century crowd.

Defoe is careful to show the colonies in a favorable light, and he is informed enough to set his novels in the colonies where land was most easily obtained. Although without amenities, the characters live almost as they might in England. Defoe includes no threatening Indians and gives no sense of the wilderness or, compared to England, the extremes of climate. In *A Plan of the English Commerce* (1728), Defoe described the North American colonies as "wild," "barren," and "inhospitable," and the Indians as fierce, treacherous, "bloody and merciless" (228–29). His *Atlas Maritimus* (1728) adds that the Indians were "gigantick," carried seven- to eight-foot-long bows, and resisted all friendly overtures (294). Although Maryland and Virginia planters routinely allowed a three-hour midday break in summer, thousands died of the heat anyway,[10] yet Jack never mentions the heat and humidity of the Virginia summer or the damp cold of winter. With his background, Jack might not be expected to complain about the diet or the limited selection of consumer goods, but Moll had learned to appreciate fine clothes.

Defoe presents transportation as both opportunity and the means to break an addictive pattern. Moll and Jack, and other characters in both books, find it to be a new chance. Had Moll's husband not been her brother, she might have lived as peaceful and productive a life as her mother had. Jack's experience reflects, perhaps, Defoe's opinion that the colonies offered men greater opportunities and benefits. Sold like any other transported person, he can count on "the custom of the country." The captain tells Jack that means he will be given land, and his master does provide 300 acres and forty or fifty pounds. In fact, Defoe was exaggerating the benefits of transportation. The custom of the country was an increasingly formal body of legislature governing the lives of "white servants." These laws specified the terms of those arriving without indentures or convictions, assured their masters' legal right, for instance, to sell them and forbid marriage, and gave them some rights, such as the capacity to sue. At the time Jack was a servant, the grant at the end of service was only fifty shillings and ten bushels of corn, no land at all. Indentured servants, however, could learn trades and some, like Jack, extended their terms with their masters in order to learn more. New research in the records in Bristol, Liverpool, and London has revealed that many Englishmen in Defoe's time believed that the "custom of the country" was a guarantee of a grant of land. The most common figure cited is fifty acres, probably because that had been the amount given in the "headrights" established by the Virginia Company in 1619 to encourage settlements. Such grants, however, were ended long before Defoe was born. That Defoe may have shared a common misapprehension means that he cannot be so easily accused of a very serious misrepresentation of the advantages of transportation. Unfortunately, Defoe does not mention the custom of the country in his nonfiction works, and no one knows what he really knew.

Defoe illustrates how ordinary Jack is by describing the arrival of a group of felons at the plantation where he works; among them is at least one who has had a career almost exactly like Jack's. The master's speech about the mercy of the change in their sentences, the opportunity they now have, and the custom of helping them start their own farms after serving their terms touches Jack deeply and rehearses the purpose and benefits of England's policy. Defoe repeatedly refers to the men as having the chance to "begin the World again" and promises that "no Diligent Man" can fail to prosper. As Jack says, "a Transported Felon, is . . . a much happier Man, than the most prosperous untaken Thief in the Nation." Notably, half of Defoe's first six novels show their characters' prosperity based upon New World plantations.

In books like *Atlas Maritimus,* Defoe surveyed the globe, determined what each part of the world had to offer, drew the lines of the spokes of the wheel, and set priorities for his countrymen.

He urged the establishment of new settlements and colonies as well as improving territory they already held. North America, in spite of its relative barrenness, had a high priority because England was nearly without competitors for land, and "a Fundamental" of improving trade was the establishment of additional colonies where "People may plant and settle." They would become consumers and producers. He saw great promise in this "uninhabited and uncultivated" land. Not only was it fertile and level but in a temperate climate, perfect for the English constitution and "for the Production of . . . all the most useful Product [*sic*] of the Earth . . . much beyond any part of the yet inhabited Quarter of the World call'd *America*."[11]

Defoe developed a picture of England becoming the richest, most powerful nation on earth through trade. He reminded his countrymen, "the rising greatness of the *British* nation is not owing to war and conquests, to enlarging its dominion by the sword, or subjecting the people of other countries to our power; but it is owing to trade." In the aftermath of the disappointing Treaty of Utrecht, Defoe's countrymen could hardly disagree. He returned to the arguments of his 1712 pamphlets and reminded people how necessary peace was for a flourishing trade and that the longest purse, not the longest sword, wins wars. Conquest, he reminded them, is "a Thing attended with Difficulty, Hazard, Expence, and a Possibility of Miscarriage." In *A General History of Discoveries* (1725–26), he argued that war, tyranny, and ambition beggar the world. Defoe imagined the produce of the world flowing into London to be redistributed and, of course, augmented with English goods and produce. Books like *A Plan of the English Commerce* and *Atlas Maritimus* target countries and products and challenge Englishmen to develop trade with them. Defoe's plan included establishing England's commercial independence; very high on his list of priorities, therefore, was getting timber, hemp, turpentine, resin, and masts from the American colonies rather than from the Baltic and Scandinavian countries. That shipbuilding and repair had to depend on these fractious countries alarmed him. To realize these ambitions, Defoe and many people of his time recognized that the population of the colonies had to be rapidly increased.

Moll Flanders, then, is more than a good story; it is also a study of a criminal mind and propaganda for contemporary policies. When Defoe began writing novels, he was an exceptionally experienced author, journalist, economic analyst, and political controversialist, and it should be no surprise that elements of these occupations find their way into the book. And, of course, he had been in prison at least six times. *Moll Flanders* is the earliest detailed study we have of the London underworld and of the social and psychological forces that incline human beings to crime. As Defoe drew upon the form of the criminal lives, he spun out an engrossing tale greatly enriched with his own reflections and experiences. The result is one of the best-known literary criminals in the world.

CHAPTER 7

Moll, Romantic Narrator

Like so many eighteenth-century novelists, Defoe used the first-person point of view for *Moll Flanders*. In other words, the narrator (in this case, Moll) tells her own story. Everything we know she tells us, and we see every event and every other character through her eyes. This point of view has obvious limitations—exposition of useful information that would not be available to the narrator, change of location, simultaneous events, and even descriptions of the narrator can be awkward or incredible. When done well, however, this technique gives individuality and immediacy to the story. Readers can feel that they have encountered a lively personality. As the novel has evolved, writers and critics have recognized the importance of the form's psychological aspects and the crucial requirement that great novels have great characters. Another novelist, William H. Gass, describes the creation of character as "not, mind you, an easy thing: rather as difficult as the whole art itself, since, in a way, it *is* the whole art: to fasten in the memory of the reader, like a living presence, some bright human image."[1] As

On the simplest—and most important—level, Defoe succeeds. Those who read the novel never forget Moll. He manages to make us forget that her story is, at least, improbable in places. In spite of the fact that she does despicable, shocking things, readers usually like her. A bigamist many times over who becomes a thief and preys on the unfortunate, the struggling, and the innocent, Moll still manages to light up the dark, violent world in which she lives. Defoe interests us in the life of someone very unlike ourselves. He holds us with her adventures and tells a good story.

On another level, however, Defoe's achievement has been debated, and critical articles with titles like "Moll's Muddle" still appear.[2] The problem is quite simple: Defoe appears to be asking the reader to separate what Moll does from what she is, to distinguish between actor and action and excuse the actor. Experience makes us aware of, first, how hard that is with real people and, second, raises the questions of whether it should be done and, if so, in what circumstances. Is Defoe telling us that it should be done? What is his judgment of Moll Flanders? In fact, what is "the theme," his message? These last questions may tell us more about critics than about the novel, and some people would ask why such demands are being made. In Anglo-American criticism, however, moral seriousness and profundity have been demanded of novels that are called "great." Authors have been expected to develop a worthy value system and to evoke laudatory judgments. At some times in our history, "poetic justice," the good rewarded and the bad punished, has been expected. For many, a book's moral vision and its possible exemplary effects outweighed any artistic merits that it might have.

Interesting people—and characters—often call forth strong reactions, positive and negative, and it is a tribute to Defoe's art that Moll has the vitality and credibility to do so. Great literature is never one-dimensional, and it resists reduction to "the theme" or "a meaning." Rather, readers can come back and back to the text and find more there—more to perceive, to consider, and to debate. Different parts may speak to different ages. What reader or critic would ever say that every aspect of George Eliot's

Middlemarch or Stephen Crane's *Red Badge of Courage* had been mastered? Should *Moll Flanders* be ranged with texts whose elusiveness is one of their greatest strengths? Or did Defoe try to get his message across in a subtle way and not quite pull it off? Did he botch the job and give us a confusing, rather meaningless character? Is he immoral and insensitive to Moll's ethical depravity? These are extreme ways to ask the questions that have arisen, but they represent the positions people have taken on *Moll Flanders.*

This issue has been somewhat complicated by the fact that Defoe provides a preface written by a fictional persona who had "edited" Moll's story, and this preface casts doubt on Moll's repentance and perhaps even on the moralizing in the narrative. It says,

> It is true, that the original of this Story is put into new Words, and the Stile of the famous Lady we here speak of is a little alter'd, particularly she is made to tell her own Tale in modester Words than she told it at first; the Copy which came first to Hand having been written in language more like one still in *Newgate,* than one grown Penitent and Humble, as she afterwards pretends to be.
>
> The Pen employ'd in finishing her Story, and making it what you now see it to be, has had no little difficulty to put it into a Dress fit to be seen, and to make it speak Language fit to be read. (1)

It goes on to say that "she liv'd it seems, to be very old; but was not so extraordinary a Penitent as she was at first" (5). This preface adds yet another layer to what is already a double perspective. Moll, as the retrospective, professedly repentant narrator, had already "edited" her remembered life when the preface-writer got the manuscript. How sincere, then, are the moral statements intended to be? How much regret is Moll intended to feel? In fact, though, how important is the preface-writer? The reader probably forgets this preface almost immediately and the fact that the pretense of the discovered manuscript was already a conventional way to make the book more appealing and acceptable further diminishes its significance.

These questions arise largely because our society and novel criticism have traditionally valued content over form. The statements on the issue to be found in important books suggest that Defoe violated expectations and was perceived to fail as an artist. Some found Moll "untouched" by her criminal career and this presentation unpleasantly unrealistic; others described her as "cynically dishonest," "having a diseased mind," or "depraved."[3] In their search for form and pattern, some highlighted the book's divergence from, for example, spiritual autobiography. But in his *Rise of the Novel,* Ian Watt reminded us that Defoe faced what "was then new and has since remained the central problem of the novel: how to impose a coherent moral structure on narrative without detracting from its air of literal authenticity." He concludes that Defoe failed to provide either a "moral or formal pattern" (117, 131). Another critic complained that Defoe's "carefully defined ironic perspective succumbs to the formlessness of Moll's mind," perhaps because Defoe failed "to define any moral world that exists outside her consciousness."[4]

Moll's "consciousness," however, includes a moral world, and the fact that English people in Defoe's time were overwhelmingly Protestant and largely in agreement with the Bible's code of ethics meant that the real social context would have supplied the coherent moral structure that we require from contemporary novelists. To subscribe to a moral code, of course, is not necessarily to practice it or to refuse to admit extenuating circumstances. The Bible itself has contradictions. For instance, one of the Ten Commandments is "Thou shall not kill," yet the Old Testament is full of battles fought by the godly in apparently approved causes. The problem with the narrator in *Moll Flanders* is not, then, the lack of a moral framework by which the reader can judge the character's actions. Rather it is the way the narrator appears to feel about her actions and the way she makes the reader feel. Moll is a master at separating what she has done from her essential self. In fact, she usually laments her crimes as sins *and* as threats to this self. She does not want her illegal actions to become the expressions of her inner being.

Denial of the relationship between action and self is not enough, however. When Moll abandons her children repeatedly, when she milks additional money from her lover in Bath, when she treats the banker as she does, and when she robs the unfortunate and continues to steal when she is no longer in need, the reader agrees with her own diagnosis: she has become a hardened woman. As a penitent, she might be expected to look on this time as the reader does, and many feel that she is not sufficiently appalled and contrite. Christian teaching, however, would say that she has put these sins behind her, feels forgiven, and now sees them in a detached way. In fact, more than the crimes themselves, the descriptions of how easily she rationalized her sins and how quickly she stopped thinking about them may make the case that she was hardened. Restitution could have been made for the crimes, but her "consciousness" required repentance.

A number of forces counteract each other in *Moll Flanders* and complicate any attempt to locate a single moral judgment of Moll. In the first place, the proportionally large amount of purely secular narrative works against the asserted spiritual theme. The preface, the beginning, and intermittent interjections lead us to expect the themes and rhetoric of a religious book. Because of the strength and consistency of these elements in didactic literature like the spiritual autobiography, reader expectations are especially strong. Thus, the subordination or even absence of such aspects casts doubts on the importance or even sincerity of those religious elements that are included.

In the second place, a number of factors put our human sympathies at odds with our moral judgments.[5] Moll repeatedly asks the reader to imagine not just her situation but her feelings of desperation and anxiety. Repeatedly, bad, *accidental* things happen to her, and she starts over without bitterness or anger. Infinitely resilient and resourceful, she evokes admiration as often as she does amazement and more often than she does aversion. Finally, clever but nonviolent criminals fascinate more ordinary and conforming people who feel a complex blend of fear and admiration, who simultaneously root for their capture and for one more daring success, and who understand yet deplore motive. The novel, unlike life, has often been expected to leave the reader feeling that a moral judgment and punishment have been rendered; *Moll Flanders* does not satisfy this desire.

Although recent critics have found greatness in the moral ambiguity of the character and her world and judged them "realistic," interpretations of the book's meaning and explanations of our enjoyment continue to be offered. In every age there are books that manage to set a sparkling face in a darkly rendered, harshly realistic world. They tell grim truths that must be admitted, yet they weave elements into the plot that transform the recollection of the experience of the novel as a whole. The work of Jane Austen has this ability. Against all odds, Elizabeth Bennett, who has refused to face the grim prospects for a woman in her situation who turns down marriage offers, marries Darcy, and *Pride and Prejudice* becomes a happy book. In *Emma* even the minor characters are tipped with this golden paint. As Knightley says of Frank Churchill, "he has used everybody ill—and they are all delighted to forgive him. —He is a fortunate man indeed!" *Moll Flanders* is such a book.

Like Austen's books, it includes elements of the romance and traces of the romantic protagonist. Its cheerful, resolute heroine goes out to conquer a world of obstacles. Originally, romances were adventure stories with something of the improbable and marvellous. Heroes performed amazing feats, and their hardships ended in triumph and happiness. Although satires of romances and ridicule of books with incidents of "knight errantry" existed in Defoe's time, the term "romantic" referred neutrally to events that were more likely to happen in romance than in life.

The careful insertion of such elements indulges the reader's delight with wish-fulfillment.

From the beginning Moll casts herself as heroine and at a very young age names the quest that will give form to her narrative— the desire to achieve economic independence as a "gentlewoman." This quest seems natural and simple today, but in Defoe's time the laughter of the village women appropriately expressed its difficulty. Women of the late seventeenth and early eighteenth centuries had few ways to earn a living. The most plentiful work was for domestics and prostitutes. Some found work in the large textile industry, but these jobs as spinners, weavers, and seamstresses, like the places women held in small stores, print shops, and coffee houses, usually went to family members, not outsiders like Moll. Conditions in these occupations were harsh. Many domestics received board but no wages and had no day off; laundry women and kitchen workers did physical labor, especially lifting, that would strain a strong man; milliners often went blind by thirty.

Moll's quest is both material and psychological; thus after the adventures, or *agon*, the crucial battle appropriately takes place in Newgate Prison where Moll "degenerated into stone, . . . turn'd first stupid and senseless, and then brutish and thoughtless, and at last raving mad as any of them" (242). She nearly surrenders her personality as well as all chance to save her body and soul. Newgate provides the culminating test and life-or-death struggle (*pathos*) for Moll: "*Newgate*; that horrid Place! my very blood chills at the mention of its Name; the Place where so many of my Comrades had been lock'd up, and from whence they went to the fatal Tree; the Place where my Mother suffered so deeply, where I was brought into the World, and from whence I expected no Redemption, but by an infamous Death: To conclude, the Place that had so long expected me, and which with so much Art and Success I had so long avoided" (273). Here she sketches in the sad associations of the place, and, like so many heroes of Christian and pagan myth acknowledges that this combat was her destiny. Like Jonah, Oedipus, and Sir Gawain, she comes to the adversary who had "long expected" her. Here she demonstrates that her actions have not expressed her nuclear self. In her concern for Mother Midnight's grief, her pity for Jemy, her acceptance of her guilt, and her gratitude to the young minister, she demonstrates her good heart. She could sink temporarily to the level of the "Newgate-bird," but at the brink of the abyss, she sees Jemy and blames herself: "My Temper was touch'd before, the harden'd wretch'd boldness of Spirit, which I had acquir'd in the Prison abated, and conscious Guilt began to flow in my Mind: In short, I began to think, and to think is one real Advance from Hell to Heaven . . . he that is restor'd to his Power of thinking, is restor'd to himself" (281). She rejects the state of mind exhibited by the hardened wretches around her as she had rejected the state of the desperate people in the Mint, and accepts the idea that she will probably be hanged. But there is a happy ending. Moll and Jemy have a pleasant voyage to the new world, riches seem to shower on them, Moll is united with her son who is loving and generous, and they return to England to live in prosperity and peace. When she stands triumphantly in Virginia, husband and son beside her, she realizes the stature of heroine, a conquering figure, in the reader's eyes as well as her own. The Greeks would call this part *anagnorisis*. Even though this conclusion is highly improbable, readers would be shocked were the book to end with Moll leaving for the death cart and Tyburn.

The romance elements in the book are too strong for such an ending, and the novel conforms too well to the pattern of most romances. Moll's babyhood is as strange and wonderful as any hero's. Birth in Newgate and travel with gypsies precede a more ordinary interval as a parish child, but even this realistic episode includes a miracle of its own. As a young child, Moll has been sure that she could never survive the life laid out for parish children. Support for such children ended when they were seven or eight, and they were put to service. As helpers to maids, cooks, washerwomen, and other domestics, they lived a hard life, and only the most fortunate were able to learn to cook or sew well enough to escape a life of manual labor. It was not uncommon for children so young to be put to work. Even in stable families, children as young as Moll were employed. In places like Colchester, seven was the age when children ordinarily began to work and "earn significant wages" by spinning and carding in the clothing trade, and girls were usually sent out to work earlier than boys.[6] Moll escapes this mind-numbing life of drudgery by managing to persuade her "nurse," the woman paid to keep her, to let her stay, and she does needlework diligently to contribute to her keep.

In fact, the perspective of the romance allows us to cast society, or perhaps more specifically patriarchal society, as the adversary as Moll struggles against the destiny it expects for her. The older brother in the Colchester family with whom she goes to live represents another social attitude and expectation. He assumes he can seduce her and then easily dispose of her. He succeeds, but we hear the story from her point of view: she begins with the delight and wonder of his love and ends with a familiar tale of betrayal. Most romances include an episode in which the breaking of a sexual barrier marks the end of youth and innocence, and that happens here. When she undertakes the adventures that make up the majority of any romance, she has learned some of society's mores and attempts to practice them. She knows her position. Women were expected to marry. In addition to the economic imperatives, the culture believed that woman's destiny, her place in life, was marriage and motherhood. The most important thing a woman did was marry, because her husband could make her utterly miserable or content, economically secure or subject to uncertainty and vicissitude resulting from his extravagance, business failures, or whims. Moll comes out of the Colchester experience intent on letting her head, not her heart, dictate her actions, and the parade of fortune-hunting men and scheming women she meets appears to confirm the insignificance of love. Her career as a thief includes satiric elements aimed at exposing some of the similarities between trade and crime. Moll leads officials to a stash of illegal, smuggled cloth and accepts a reward. Mother Midnight's house works like a good business, and shop-owners and employees are as heartless and rapacious as the robbers Moll meets on the street. Above all, Defoe's language draws the respectable and criminal worlds together. For instance, of her stolen goods, Moll says, "I was now at a loss for a market for my goods" and that she made "several good bargains" in carelessly attended shops.

Defoe's novel is set firmly in his time and draws upon another common opinion of the time: that economic considerations had become too important in courtships. Defoe and others, such as the Anglican clergyman William Fleetwood, insisted that marriage should not be a cold-blooded contract negotiated by families intent on improving their positions or fortunes. The fact that playwrights and novelists of the time frequently used this situation as the central conflict of their works argues that the subject was of great interest and some controversy. Playwrights like Aphra Behn, Thomas Southerne, and George Farquhar showed the miseries of such marriages, and, of course, Samuel Richardson turned a daughter's aversion to the man her family selected for her into one of the greatest novels of the century, *Clarissa*.

Moll's marriages and near-marriages illustrate the dreams—and the snares—associated with courtship, but Moll is more than a fortune-hunter. She seeks a lasting love, a companionate and sexual relationship. When she gets involved with the older brother, she is making a young woman's mistake. Young men and women in Defoe's time usually married in their mid-twenties and were expected to set up a separate household at once. It is natural, therefore, at first for marriage to be in the back, not in the forefront of the mind of a woman as young as Moll was in Colchester. The flirtation and conversation they share leads to exploitation and heartbreak for Moll even as its fullness illustrates that Moll had the right idea but the wrong man. She had, after all, enjoyed his conversation, his charm, his relatively cultured life, and his body. Moll never entirely surrenders her hope for these things within marriage. Defoe's *Religious Courtship* (1722) and his second (or two-part) *Family Instructor* (1718) had been largely devoted to advice on how to select a good husband. *Religious Courtship,* published the same year as *Moll Flanders,* had included a near-catechism for women to ask their suitors, and the episode in which Moll helps a friend find out about the man she loves by spreading rumors about him includes highly similar material. *Conjugal Lewdness* (1727) dramatizes Defoe's belief in the necessity of mutual friendship, respect, and romantic love for happy marriages. In fact, one modern critic has argued that readers in Defoe's time would have seen Moll as a negative example, and her series of disastrous marriages as "appropriate punishment" for her crass, loveless marriages.[7]

Moll has, in fact, been unable to take her own advice. Immediately after she helps her friend check on the suitor's character and financial state, she marries the Virginia planter, "the best humour'd Man that ever Woman had" (82) and later Jemy, the nearly penniless Irishman. Impetuous, passionate, and self-gratifying, her heart overrules her preachings of caution and establishes a consistency of character seen in her impulsive thefts. For all her hard and cynical statements, she falls in love repeatedly. Always the optimist in love, she is repeatedly disappointed.

The conclusion of *Moll Flanders* rejects the outcome determined by society. In Newgate and Virginia, Moll finally reasserts a set of values at odds with the gamesmanship she has learned. In spite of all her resolutions to avoid "that cheat called love," she had loved Jemy, spent with him what time they could afford, and, years later, still opens her heart to him. Her self and her actions cohere, and she is reunited with the man whom she found most compatible and fun. When she writes her autobiography, she concludes as most romances do, with the contemplation of her adventures. Her narrative may not deliver poetic justice, but it provides a model for forging a new life—something better than the rendering of judgment and the carrying out of punishment.

Some of Defoe's originality as a fiction writer comes from his blending of such apparently incompatible genres as the romance and the criminal life. As a professional writer with at least forty years' experience, he well understood how important it was to appeal to readers. The growth of the middle class, with its power to purchase entertaining books, was shaping literary publication as never before, and he catered to their interests—both social and literary. For instance, women criminals had always been popular subjects because of their novelty and, because more women were being prosecuted for crimes, they became more frequent subjects. Moreover, he made Moll appealing to the increasing numbers of women readers as well as to those who would have found her story appealing as criminal narrative. Moll's girlhood ambitions, her first romance, and her tragicomic search for a husband, as well as the descriptions of her disguises and her problem pregnancies, could not be found even in the longest criminal lives, but they were elements common to some of the shorter fiction of the period. Many scholars of rogue literature have noted how Moll's first affair sets Defoe apart from all earlier writers.[8]

Above all, Defoe exhibits masterful control of tone. When Moll is little more than a thieving machine she steals a horse and cannot think of anything to do with it. This essentially comic episode breaks an increasingly judgmental reaction and returns us to the position of amused and amazed readers. The fact that Moll calls herself harsher names than we would also acts paradoxically to soften the reader's opinion of her. When she begins to call herself a whore, the reader is acutely conscious of the fact that she has been a young girl seduced by a man who looks worse page by page. He had promised her marriage, and, furthermore, at that time engagements were binding contracts, and premarital sex between the affianced was fairly common. Not only does her seducer palm her off on his brother, but he cruelly jokes that she is ill because in love and even tells his brother, "I deal in no such Ware, I have nothing to say to no Mrs. Betty's." She calls herself a cheat when she tricks men to marry her, but they are fortune-hunters and pretenders, too. By the time she begins to steal, the reader has observed the predatory, harsh world in which she lives and has largely accepted her desperation. Moreover, Defoe makes it clear that Moll often preys on the "sins" of others—vanity, lasciviousness, and avarice.

Although Moll is committing both crimes and sins, she is teaching a lesson to families that allow nine-year-olds in St. James Park alone with gold watches and pearl necklaces, to people who walk in crowds with ostentatious ornaments, to old gentlemen who pick up women at the Bartholomew Fair and then have cause to fear the pox, and to men who prey upon fortunes only to find themselves married to poor women.

Like all popular fiction, *Moll Flanders* has allowed readers to escape their mundane lives, vicariously experience new things, and indulge in improbable adventures, but, also, like popular fiction, the book reinforces traditional, even conservative mores. Moll ends with Jemy, a legitimate husband and the man she has loved most. Still, it is not marriage and a man that give Moll security but thrift and ingenuity as a criminal and fresh opportunities in the New World. She has realized her dream and succeeded in her quest.

CHAPTER
8

Minor
Characters

Although Moll Flanders dominates this book, Defoe surrounds her with a rich and diverse group of minor characters. He includes nearly two hundred of them, and they represent a number of social classes and life-styles, and collectively provide part of the setting and emotional context for Moll's life and actions. Many of the characters are shadowy figures like Moll's Colchester "nurse"; others, like the seducing older brother, are already literary stereotypes. All, however, are important for what they mean to Moll.

Some of Moll's appeal certainly comes from the fact that she is a woman, and Defoe gradually deprives her of the kinds of support women in the eighteenth-century ordinarily had. As the child of a felon, she was separated in infancy from her mother. As a parish child, she tried to cast as "mother" the woman employed to keep her and other children like her. Moll's "nurse" is a neat, sober, thrifty, pious woman who kept a little school, and Moll is happy and well-cared for until the nurse dies, soon after Moll's fourteenth birthday. By that time, Moll has internalized an ideal of neatness, civility, and good management with the help of this woman who had been forced to support herself. Kind as she is to Moll, though, this nurse has accepted all of Moll's wages and gifts from her and she benefits from the notoriety Moll gives her. She is quick to repeat Moll's naive statements and to laugh at her with the other women. When she dies, a daughter comes, and Moll's former home is "swept . . . all away at once." In fact, the daughter's joke, "that the little Gentlewoman might set up for her self," might suggest recognition of Moll's delusions as well as jealousy.

In the nurse's home, Moll meets a stream of middle-class Colchester ladies. They come to bring sewing and mending, to select servant girls, and for vague charitable purposes. Since Moll was not born in Essex, the parish has no legal responsibility for her. The Colchester officials' placement of Moll (an action at odds with Defoe's descriptions of the heartlessness of some parishes in books such as the 1727 *Parochial Tyranny* and the 1728 *Augusta Triumphans*) is but one of the compliments Defoe pays the county in which he was renting land. Nevertheless, the Colchester women are condescending and, even as they make a pet of her and keep her supplied with sewing, they laugh at her.

In this sequence, Defoe sets up for the first time the complex double vision so important to the novel. Moll presents herself as singled out and petted, but the ridicule of other characters punctures her pretensions and emphasizes her illusions. More subtle yet are the comparisons and contrasts set up between Moll and the other characters. These juxtapositions consistently reveal the self-interest of characters who represent more familiar and respectable positions and occupations than Moll's. Many of these characters are thought to be exemplary, and they think highly of themselves; thus, Defoe deepens his themes of the discrepancies between appearance and reality, and the elusiveness of truth, and the universality of such human characteristics as self-deception and egoism.

Moll's second home is with a typical Colchester middle-class family, one that could have come out of one of Defoe's conduct books like *The Family Instructor* (1715) or *Religious Courtship*

(1722). This family has several daughters and two sons, and within the household Moll considers herself a vicarious daughter. In this comfortable, affluent family, the children have "masters" who give them lessons in dancing, singing, playing the spinet and harpsichord, and other social skills. Moll says, "I learn'd by Imitation and enquiry, all that they learn'd by Instruction and Direction." Class distinctions are highly evident, for they call her "Betty," the generic name the century gave house maids. Soon the children, all of marriageable age or close to it, begin to discuss her marriage prospects with due note of her position. When they attach "Mrs." to "Betty" (people then referred to women above a certain age, married or unmarried, as "Mrs."), they are acknowledging her adulthood and assigning it to her at a younger age than to themselves, probably because the lower classes married somewhat younger than the more affluent. And the older brother seduces her. Fiction, biography, and legal history all tell us that housemaids were considered fair game, and later plays and novels are full of allusions and stories of such seductions or rapes. Samuel Richardson based the entire plot of his popular novel, *Pamela* (1741), on the story of a resisting servant girl.

This older brother displays the carelessness, arrogance, and insensitivity of his class, and the story of the naive, trusting girl and the lover was already a cliché by Defoe's time. He knows that the tradition of primogeniture will make him the heir to almost everything his parents have, and he believes that the servant girl, Moll, is insignificant. What follows is predictable, but Defoe surpasses many such stories by adding emotionally realistic dialogue, a particularly macabre twist, and major preparation for plot developments. Defoe even assures that the reader will understand the situation, for Moll, as retrospective narrator, tells us at the beginning, "Mrs. *Betty* was in Earnest, and the Gentleman was not." The brother flatters her, gives her gold, and promises to marry her, and she believes he loves her. Her own high opinion of her beauty, talents, and charm combined with her youthful trust and inexperience allow her to believe him. They meet clandestinely; he continues to give her gifts and make her promises. When complications arise, of course he tries to end the relationship.

The twist Defoe gives this old story is to have the younger brother fall in love with her and court her seriously. Unlike his brother, he does so openly and pugnaciously; the family is enraged at what they consider to be a scheming, ambitious servant and discuss "turning her out," which is, significantly, the terminology used when an unsatisfactory servant was fired. Moll, of course, is terrified since she has nowhere to go and no way to earn a living. She apparently innocently suggests to the older brother that they end the uproar by telling the family that she is promised to him; then he is horrified. He advises her to marry his brother and breaks off the affair with the excuse that he will be disinherited. The arguments they have capture the pain of relationships ended without mutual consent. Moll pleads, begs, and reminds him of promises made; the brother finds the recriminations uncomfortable and tries to avoid additional unpleasantness. Sometimes he talks with sensitivity, and sometimes he is cruel enough to joke about her with his family. Moll is heartbroken, and Defoe gives her several emotionally powerful lines. At sixty-two, Defoe can still write the most agonizing questions about love: "Can you bid me cease loving you . . . ? is it in my Power think you to make such a Change at Demand?" Moll asks. But, faced with being turned out in the street, she marries the younger brother. The outcome is grim, for she confesses, "I never was in Bed with my Husband, but I wish'd my self in the Arms of his Brother." The poet John Masefield compares this part of the novel with the universally praised Newgate sequence: "the ghastly naturalness of her seduction and the horror of the days passed by her in the condemned cell haunt the memory forever."[1]

After the death of this first husband, Moll remains in London where they had settled, and the cast of characters expands rapidly. The pattern of relationships that Defoe sets up shows Moll tending to turn to women for advice and, for much of the book, to men with the hope of economic security. Her experience with women is uniformly better than with men. After her Colchester nurse, she finds a number of women who help her, and they are a varied group. For instance, the affluent mother of the family in Colchester treated Moll much more fairly than many women in her situation might have. She did not want her son to marry a "beggar" and suspected Moll of being a "snare," but she carefully waited until Moll's health was better before she mentioned the family's plan to have her move, and she took Moll's denials of involvement with Robin, the younger brother, seriously. Convinced of Moll's sincerity and urged by the older brother as well as Robin, she agrees to the marriage. Moll's first London intimates, a widow and the wife-to-be of sea captains, help initiate her into the London marriage market, and the second helps her trick the Virginia planter into marrying her. All three of these women reinforce the theme that money is now a preoccupation in proposals, and the younger woman's experiences mirror the strategic maneuvering and sexual warfare of Moll's first relationship. This woman has wanted to find out if the man who courted her was as prosperous as he claimed, and of good character, but her inquiries angered him. Through an elaborate plot devised by Moll, the woman finds out what she wants to know and the couple is reconciled.

These three women have no names, and very little other than their domestic and economic situations is known. They show, however, the positions women had in society and what kinds of influence they had. As the matriarch of a large family in which the father was preoccupied with his work, the Colchester woman has great authority. As women with comfortable fortunes, the two London women have the means of marrying; their power clearly comes, however, from money, and at least one must use trickery to protect and advance herself. All three testify to the absolute, ultimate significance marriage had for women at that time. More important to the Colchester mother than Moll's good character and all of her talents, more important than her son's affections, is the fact that Moll has no money. Defoe repeats observations he made about marriage in his conduct books, "Women have ten Thousand times the more Reason to be wary and backward, by how much the hazard of being betray'd is the greater."

Moll's next female mentor is, ironically, her own mother. Moll can be seen to be seeking a mother throughout the book, but when she does find her mother it is part of a terrible revelation: she has accidentally married her own brother. Moll's mother is one of the most developed characters in the book, and her story resembles in part that of another character of Defoe's, a wife of Colonel Jack. As a transported felon, she had been bound to a planter. After years of hard work, her widowed master married her, and she in turn was widowed but continued to improve the plantation where she now lives in the comfort of the colonial equivalent of the Colchester matron. Justly proud of her rehabilitation and eager to explain how she succeeded, she offers yet another version of the independent, successful woman. When she learns that Moll is her daughter, she makes her will in such a way as to assure an independent fortune for Moll.

Back in England, Moll has a series of new female mentors, all single and all independent. Some, like the Bath landlady, act rather like procuresses and gain from their association with Moll; this landlady, for instance, introduces Moll to the prosperous man who will support her for six years, thereby getting board and gifts for herself. Another, the woman who takes Moll to Lancashire, has been paid £100 by Jemy, her former lover, to help him trick Moll into marriage. Moll's most memorable friend is the woman brought to her sick bed by yet one more landlady who thinks she knows what Moll needs. She introduces Mother Midnight to Moll with the words, "I believe this Lady's Trouble is of a kind that is pretty much in your way, and therefore if you can do anything for her, pray do, for she is a very civil Gentlewoman" (161). Once again the community of women closes around Moll.

The landlady's words, however, would have had chilling associations to the eighteenth-century reader. Her name explains her trade—bawd, midwife, creature of the night, perhaps abortionist and infanticide. Whatever a woman in trouble might need, she would supply. A perfect name, "Mother" identified her proprietary relationship to her house and the women who came there to board, to bear children, or to do business.[2] "Midnight" reached into the deepest recesses of English folklore and associated her with the mysterious, the uncanny, and the evil. The circumstances in which she is summoned to see Moll obviously suggest the special, secret knowledge that many believed midwives had. Woman's body and especially her reproductive organs had had mythical power and special mystery since the beginning of time, and midwives sometimes seemed to have nearly magical power. Rumored to use drugs and charms to relieve pain and to use uncommon manual dexterity to aid the births of babies, they also seemed to have considerable opportunity to turn these beneficial skills to evil. The same drugs that could relieve might mark a baby or kill; the same hands that might deftly disengage an umbilical cord from a baby's neck might in an instant cut off the infant's air and kill before the faces of the mother's kin. Canny could slip into cunning, and swaddling into smothering. "Midnight" is the moment when time stands poised between night and morning, just as any birth in the eighteenth century poised mother and child precariously between life and death, so perilous was childbirth then. Mother Cresswell, Mother Wiseborne, Mother Osborne, Mother Needham, Mother Griffiths, Mother Burgess—the annals of London life testify to the notoriety of such real women, and even the 1706 Act against the Discharge and Murder of Bastard Children, the efforts of constables and Societies for the Reformation of Manners, and regular orders for the closing of their houses failed to diminish their trade. Mother Midnight's name and her dark hints to Moll make her somewhat more sinister than the London ladies known for their expensive bordellos, but even they were so detested that, for instance, Mother Needham died from the injuries she suffered while standing in the pillory.

Under Mother Midnight's care, Moll recovers her health and spirit, arranges to get rid of Jemy's child, and emerges ready for a respectable marriage to the bank clerk. After his death, she seeks out Mother Midnight and, once again, finds her able to take troublesome "goods" off her hands—Mother Midnight is now a "pawn broker" and can dispose of Moll's stolen property as she once did her baby. The London midwife-bawds were especially notorious for their corruption of the young, and, in fact, Mother Midnight is in reduced circumstances because a man had sued her for helping "convey away" his daughter. These women reputedly charmed young women, initiated them into their trade, and profitted. Just as Mother Cresswell had tutored Mother Wiseborne, so another mother midnight had passed her woman's secrets along to Moll's "Governess." Soon Mother Midnight introduces Moll to "a school-mistress" who teaches her to be a "compleat thief." As the language of the book draws the merchant's world and the thief's together, here Defoe imposes the midwife's on Moll's tutelage.[3] Moll says that Mother Midnight "conquer'd all my Modesty and all my Fears." She goes on to describe how she "attended [the thief to whom Mother Midnight had introduced her] some time in her Practise, just as a Deputy attends a Midwife without any Pay" and how she became wonderfully "dexterous" (201). The first theft this teacher allows Moll to try is that of a pregnant woman's watch. Defoe loved such clever games with language and situation and, after the woman is jolted and frightened, and even cries out, Moll neatly unhooks the watch and delivers the woman of her trinket (201–2).

Mother Midnight encourages, harbors, and advises Moll. Just as the bawd procures men for her harlots, Mother Midnight sets Moll up with accomplices. "I Came into a kind of League with these two, by the help of my Governess," she says of one pair, but she finds them "unhandy" and is relieved when they are hanged (209). Moll notes that she "had a new Tempter, who prompted me every Day, I mean my Governess," and Mother Midnight takes the place of the Devil in the narrative. Moll had blamed him for putting temptation in her way and even prompting her to action; now the Governess points out opportunities for crime and, like the madam of a house, expects "a good Share of the Booty" (209–10). Mother Midnight, in fact, is the real master pick-pocket and continues Moll's education until she is "the greatest Artist of my time" and could work her way "out of every danger with such dexterity" that she sees many caught and hanged during the five or six years during which she practices her trade unapprehended.

The Colchester nurse had allowed Moll to put off going to service, and her own mother had promised her an inheritance that would protect her from some of the consequences that her incestuous marriage might bring. Similarly, Mother Midnight tries to prevent the conclusion that society had written after Moll's arrest. She goes from person to person in Moll's behalf, and, like Moll's mother, faces the consequences of her own action. She sends the minister to Moll and he "breaks into her soul." He arranges for her to be transported rather than hanged. The Governess makes her transportation easier and becomes her banker. In turn, she becomes a penitent and dies, we are told, an honest woman.

The men whom Moll meets represent almost every social class and reinforce the theme that "the number of such men as an honest woman ought to meddle with is small indeed." Defoe dispenses with the Colchester older brother with a devastating moral judgment: "So naturally do Men give up Honour and Justice, and even Christianity, to secure themselves" (58). Many of the men are vain and foolish, as Moll's second husband is. He loves to dress up and even hires a coachman, postilion, footmen, and a page for their Oxford trip. Moll indulges Jemy: "I took especial care to buy for him all those things that I knew he delighted to have; as two good long Wigs, two silver-hilted Swords, . . . a fine Saddle with Holsters and Pistoles very handsome, with a Scarlet Cloak" (340). Others are weak; two die of heartbreak because they go bankrupt, and several carry on cowardly adulterous affairs. Defoe showers contempt on them all, both by their contrasts to Moll and with direct statement. When the bank clerk broods over his financial loss, she says, "the Loss fell very heavy on my Husband, yet it was not so great neither, but that if he had had Spirit and Courage to have look'd his Misfortunes in the Face, his Credit was so good, that as I told him, he would easily recover it; for to sink under Trouble is to double the Weight" (189). Of the man who picks Moll up at the Fair, she writes, "There is nothing so absurd, so surfeiting, so ridiculous as a Man heated by Wine in his Head, and a wicked Gust in his Inclination together; . . . and he acts Absurdities even in his View; such is Drinking more, when he is Drunk already; picking up a common Woman, without any regard to what she is, or who she is, whether Sound or Rotten, Clean or Unclean . . . such a Man is worse than Lunatick" (226).

To some extent all of the male characters are types, but just as Defoe could add flashes of originality to the minor female characters, so he does to the male, and he is especially good at exploiting the popular opinions of these types as he does with Mother Midnight. Jemy is the most obvious example. A dashing, improvident, slick-tongued Irishman, he amuses Moll, and she find him "the most entertaining that ever I met with in my life before." He leaves her, but she silently calls him back, and he returns. This preternatural event, perhaps, shows the harmony between them. They live together as long as they can afford to, and he returns to his criminal life. Years later in Newgate, Moll compares him to the famous highwaymen Captain James Hind, James Whitney, and the Golden Farmer (John Bennet), and that associates him with the most romanticized of all eighteenth-century criminals. Even though highwaymen were hated and feared, they already had some of the reputation of the kings of the road. Alexander Smith's *A Compleat History of the Lives and Robberies of the Most Notorious Highway-Men, Footpads, Shop-Lifts, and Cheats of Both Sexes* (1719) had mythologized their lives, and highwaymen were becoming the glamorous, solitary, even courtly gentlemen thieves.[4] The red cape and flashy sword and pistols Moll buys Jemy for his retired life in Virginia fit the image of the dashing figure with little practical value.

Defoe is too serious and too realistic to let Jemy become a

fantasy figure. Jemy expresses some of the pessimism found in other male characters. Moreover, Jemy objects to going to the colonies; he tries to persuade Moll to try her scheme in Ireland, and in Newgate expresses his anxiety and preference for the land he knows. His objections to the colonies are snobbish. He says that "Servitude and hard Labour were things Gentlemen could never stoop to," but Moll persuades him that their money will keep them comfortable.

All in all, Defoe makes Jemy into a fairly satisfactory romantic hero. He courts Moll with skill and genuine affection, enjoys her company and does what he can for her, and finally retires in contentment with her. Their stories have much in common, and several scenes between them have tenderness and gentle pathos. When they talk, he often puts his arms around her, and he calls her "my dear." She calls him a man of gallant spirit and describes him "as Penitent, for having put all those cheats upon me as if it had been Felony" (150–51). When they meet again in prison, he says, "Unhappy Couple!" and they comfort each other. "Let us compare our Sorrows," she offers (297–98). When he finds out about her incestuous marriage, he merely reproaches her for thinking she could not tell him.

The older, lascivious men were also familiar types, but Defoe manages to make them interesting. The Bath gentleman lets her know that his wife was "distemper'd in her head," and they spend their time talking in his bedroom, and even spend two years "bundling," the practice of talking or sleeping together in a bed, usually fully dressed, which was tolerated throughout the eighteenth century. She nurses him when he is sick but finally "exchang'd the Place of Friend for that unmusical harsh sounding Title of WHORE" (116). Defoe once again provides a situation in which the plot is predictable; just as the progress and conclusion of the Colchester affair was, so is her sexual relationship with the Bath gentleman and his eventual repentance. The first part of their affair is devoted to their mutual tests and dares ("he protested to me, that if he was naked in bed with me he would as sacredly preserve my virtue"), and the second to Moll's saving money "for a wet day," which she feels is sure to come. Defoe spins out the encounter with the man from Bartholomew Fair by describing the man's terrified fear of the pox and his subsequent visits to Moll. Here Mother Midnight truly acts as procuress, and his cautious defensiveness turns to renewed lascivious interest during her shrewd conversation with him.

Another group of characters reinforce the sense that Moll's world is full of self-interested cheats and opportunists. The large number of thieves, both male and female, that Moll meets seems at first to be part of an amorphous underworld, but they have an unsettling tendency to emerge briefly as individual, significant characters or to provide an undeniable likeness to a "respectable" group. Moll describes debtors in the Mint "while a Penny lasted, nay, even beyond it, endeavouring to drown their Sorrow in their Wickedness; heaping up more Guilt upon themselves, labouring to forget former things, which now it was the proper time to remember, making more Work for Repentance, and Sinning on, as a Remedy for Sin past" (65). She herself, she says, has been left by her husband "to Rob the Creditors for something to Subsist on" (62). What seems part of Moll's harshly judgmental language about herself is, in retrospect, yet another way that trade and crime are the same, and the language customarily used to obscure the similarity is stripped away. Harsh and dangerous as the streets are, the lives of the thieves seem a series of daring attempts, and success and camaraderie appear common. Dressed as a man, Moll had a partner whom she found "nimble enough" and they "grew very intimate." She describes another pair of thieves so inseparable that "they robb'd together, lay together, were taken together, and at last were hang'd together."

Inside Newgate, however, another side of this crew emerges. Again reflections on the episodes in the book take on new, deeper meanings. The number of Moll's acquaintances who have been hanged comes to emphasize the inevitability of their fate rather than the contrast to Moll's dexterity—or luck. Desperate, uneducated, besotted, and hopeless, they join a stinking, howling mob that might people Dante's Hell. Those who may have been merely dirty or "unhandy" join those who have been respectably dressed and comfortable like Moll. An eighteenth-century visitor to Newgate's ward for female felons described the place and its inhabitants:

> they knowing their Time to be short here, rather than bestow one Minute towards cleaning the same, suffer themselves to live far worse than Swine . . . the *Augean* Stable could bear no Comparison to it, for they are almost poisoned with their own Filth, and their Conversation is nothing but one continued Course of Swearing, Cursing and Debauchery, insomuch that it surpasses all Description and Belief. [The women] are worse than the worst of the Men, not only in respect to Nastiness and Indecency of living, but more especially as to their Conversation, which . . . is as prophane and wicked, as Hell itself can possibly be."[5]

Defoe captures this atmosphere dramatically. Visitors to the prison often mentioned that they nearly fainted because of the odor, and Moll is horrified at "the hellish noise, the roaring, swearing and clamour, the stench and nastiness." One of the women tells her that Newgate looked to her just as it now did to Moll, but she now dances and sings. For a short time Moll becomes like them; Newgate levels them all.

It has been said that Moll Flanders has few relationships, but over her long life, she has many, and some of them are very close. She loves a number of people well, and some return her affection. Although she seeks out people who can do things for her, she also hopes for satisfying, mutual relationships with people whose minds and manners she can enjoy. The scores of characters that populate Moll's world define it.

CHAPTER 9

Language and Style

Most of the prose fiction written at the time Defoe wrote *Moll Flanders* is in the form of authentic, personal kinds of writing. Letters, journals, memoirs, biographies, autobiographies, criminal lives, histories, and even ship's logs were published. By the time Defoe published his novels, readers already knew that some were fictional and some were not. Prefaces claimed that the authors had been eyewitnesses, that they had been told the story by a witness, or that the manuscript had been found or given to the publisher, and argued that, in each case, the circumstances strongly suggested its authenticity.

Like readers today, eighteenth-century people thought they could learn different things from nonfiction and from literary forms. They agreed that actual experience in Borneo or a real visit to Newgate Prison ought to allow the writer to include details and experiences (and even feelings) not available to the writer of fiction. Seventeenth-century writers tried to explain fiction, and their words often sound defensive, as if they are trying to justify departing from empirical, literal truth. John Bunyan in "The Author's Apology for his Book" in his *Pilgrim's Progress* listed as one of the objections made to it as "it is feigned." He goes on for more than 100 lines to justify his use of fiction. By 1722, however, people unabashedly enjoyed prose fiction, and authors had learned to incorporate pious sentiments and didactic material into the most sensational of books. Readers were to learn, for instance, from Eliza Haywood's *Love in Excess* (published in 1719, and one of the few books to rival *Robinson Crusoe* in sales) about the power and nature of love.

By the time he wrote *Moll Flanders,* Defoe was one of the most skillful propagandists in English history. He was a master at impersonating the voices of different political and religious groups, and, like Jonathan Swift, who wrote from the point of view of a patriotic Irish draper and an economic projector, he developed ways to make his prose style an important part of character creation. To succeed, such a style had to sound like that of an individual whose speech had quirks, favorite phrases, and distinctive rhythms. It had to establish and develop a relationship with the reader, and it contributed immeasurably to the reader's enjoyment. Whether one thinks that readers came to believe that Moll Flanders had been a real person who had done at least some of the things told in Defoe's book, or that her personality and adventures were "probable" enough to be acceptable to her readers, or that "a willing suspension of disbelief" happened, the language and style of the book make it acceptable to the reader who insists upon some illusion of authenticity.

A number of things make Moll's language sound "real." It can be highly specific as it names actual streets and familiar paths known to London readers, as Moll steals a variety of the items available in London shops, and as it details what Moll wore in successive disguises. This specificity and occasional mention of things in the readers' own world were familiar techniques used by writers who wanted to increase the credibility of their narratives; Aphra Behn, for example, mentioned a famous headdress in a popular play, *The Indian Queen,* in *Oroonoko.* Similarly, the narrator's claim to being an authority was common, and Moll's lectures on the marriage market and on how thieves work are of a piece with other fiction of the time.

One critic complained that Defoe's writing often sounded as if it had been written on horse back, and it does sometimes seem to bump and ramble along. One of his most characteristic modes is to spin out ideas or adventures and, in so doing, to write in what has been called an "improvisational" mode. In the words of P. N. Furbank and W. R. Owens, the feature of Defoe's style that is most striking is how a

> passage keeps taking on a new lease of life—seems again and again to be reaching its conclusion and then, with perfect but unexpected logic, manages to postpone its end. What one is witnessing is a remarkable syntactical resourcefulness on Defoe's part, and we may cling to the word "syntax," though it is straining the word to its limit. Those interpolations that keep thrusting in, saving the sentence ("paragraph"?) from expiry, are syntactically perfectly sound; the logic of the sentence's endless extension is impeccable; and in retrospect the sentence is found to be most beautifully organised and articulated."[1]

In a pseudo-autobiographical form like *Moll Flanders* this technique gives a powerfully vivid impression of a mind in motion, of a reacting, reasoning, thinking, living human being. At one point, Moll explains,

> I was now a loose unguided Creature, and had no Help, no Assistance, no Guide for my Conduct: I knew what I aim'd at, and what I wanted, but knew nothing how to pursue the End by direct means; I wanted to be plac'd in a settled State of Living, and had I happen'd to meet with a sober good Husband, I should have been as faithful and true a Wife to him as Virtue itself could have form'd: If I had been otherwise, the Vice came in always at the Door of Necessity, not at the Door of Inclination; and I understood too well, by the want of it, what the value of a settl'd Life was, to do any thing to forfeit the felicity

of it; nay, I should have made the better Wife for all the Difficulties I had pass'd thro', by a great deal; nor did I in any of the
Times that I had been a Wife, give my Husbands the least un-
easiness on account of my Behaviour. (128–29)

In this passage, Moll assesses her situation, explains what she
wants, spins out contingencies, explains her behavior, and concludes with three clauses that reinforce how highly she values the
"settled State of Living." As the sentence unfolds, she both ad-
dresses her reader fully and confidentially and appears to explore
the relationship among her desire for a settled domestic life, the
events in her life, and her decisions and moral character. Each seg-
ment of the sentence has an interest of its own, and the form as a
whole admirably suits the content.

 Moll Flanders' account purports to be a retrospect autobiography, and, again, the improvisatory sentence is an artistic choice.
It can be an efficient vehicle for summary and can juxtapose event
and feeling effectively:

> At length a new Scene open'd: There was in the House, where
> I Lodg'd, a North Country Woman that went for a Gentle-
> woman, and nothing was more frequent in her Discourse,
> than her account of the cheapness of Provisions, and the easie
> way of living in her Country; how plentiful and how cheap
> every thing was, what good Company they kept, and the like;
> till at last I told her she almost tempted me to go and live in
> her County; for I that was a Widow, tho' I had sufficient to
> live on, yet had no way of encreasing it, and that *London* was
> an expensive and extravagant Place; that I found I could not
> live here under a Hundred Pound a Year, unless I kept no
> Company, no Servant, made no Appearance, and buried my
> self in Privacy. (129)

The moment at which Moll begins to find the North Country attractive, when she is "tempted" to relocate there, interrupts the
sentence a bit and makes it take on new immediacy even as it gives

a rapid summary of the way Moll came to make the decision that would lead to her next marriage. The sentence even recaptures the personality of the woman who, after her first marriage, sought out fun-loving people and a lively society.

In fact, the prose style of *Moll Flanders* is highly efficient. When Moll robs the child who is on her way home from dancing school, she tells us how she set up the crime: "I talk'd to it, and it prattl'd to me again, and I took it by the Hand, and led it a long till I came to a pav'd alley that goes into *Bartholomew Close,* and I led it in there" (194). In addition to representing the physical distance, the space, that Moll covered, the sentence graphically illustrates how she led the child along with her conversation and by the hand. As in so many descriptions in the novel, there is a strong physicality that contributes to the realism and vividness of the scene. Moll touches things. She "thrusts against the Square of Glass" in a window in order to steal two rings; she notes that she has stolen "a Peice of fine black Lustring Silk," and thereby tells us that it was glossy and smooth. Moll is, in George A. Starr's words, in "active contact with things: having hold, giving a jostle, giving a pull, being balked, letting go."[2] Equally swiftly, she can move through different time frames and pronounce a final judgment on an incident in her life. For instance, of her incestuous marriage and life in Virginia, she says, "I could almost as willingly have embrac'd a Dog, as have let him offer any thing of that kind to me. . . . I cannot say that I was right in Point of Policy in carrying it such a length . . . but I am giving an Account of what was, not of what ought or ought not to be" (98).

Eighteenth-century literature was habitually read aloud. Many accounts of people standing on street corners listening to one of their number read the newspaper, of families reading together in the evenings, and of circles of friends gathering to read survive. In fact, eighteenth-century prose takes on a different dimension when it is read aloud; the richness of the detail and the variety of tones and rhythms suddenly become clear. Both because of the time in which it was written and as an aspect of its imitation of an autobiography, *Moll Flanders* is idiomatic, colloquial, and full of the characteristics of spoken English:

> It is enough to tell you, that as some of my worst Comrades, who are out of the Way of doing me Harm, having gone out of the World by the Steps and the String as I often expected to go, know me by the Name of *Moll Flanders;* so you may give me leave to speak of myself, under that Name till I dare own who I have been, as well as who I am.
>
> I have been told, that in one of our Neighbour Nations, whether it be *France,* or where else. (7)

Clauses like "It is enough to tell you" and "I have been told" and interjections such as "as I often expected to go" make the prose conversational and direct. Her use of euphemisms such as "having gone out of the World by the Steps and the String" for the gallows make her speech lively and, cumulatively, suggest the ways thieves deal with their fears. This passage from the opening page of the novel will be recalled in the macabre scene in which a fellow prisoner in Newgate dances and sings for Moll: "If I swing by the String,/I shall hear the Bell ring./And then there's an End of poor Jenny" (275). Moll seems to remain aware of those who are reading or hearing her story at all times. She is at pains to set the scene, to make sure that they apprehend her situation, that they understand the other characters, and that they can sympathize with her feelings and decisions. She includes such rhetorical phrases as "it is enough to tell you," "in short," and "something I must not omit." Sometimes she draws specifically upon the human feelings that she assumes readers share. Of the highwaymen in Newgate, she says, "It is not to be wonder'd that we who were Prisoners, were all desirous enough to see these brave topping Gentlemen," and of her state of mind after being sentenced to hanging, "It is rather to be thought of, than express'd what was now my Condition." The reader, then, is called upon to imagine the fullness of her entrapment and her emotional and mental life. Because she has lived in an environment that few share, she sometimes defines "hard" or "cant" words and explains in great detail how shopkeepers and watch-wearers provided the opportunities for theft. Defoe fashions her dialogue so that she seems to do so both with the pride of the initiated, knowledgeable expert and with the thoughtfulness of a good friend and storyteller. In fact, Moll comes to ally herself with the reader rather than with her former associates: At one point she remarks that she is giving information "not of the kindest Sort to the Fraternity" when she explains how to catch pickpockets.

Other stylistic devices, such as the repetition of "I say," contribute to the novel's oral quality. Moll describes the deal she struck with Mother Midnight, one she hoped would prevent the murder or mistreatment of her unborn but unwanted baby. "O Mother, *says I,* if I was but sure my little Baby would be carefully look'd to, and have Justice done it." As she relates the conversation, she repeats "says I" and "says she," and the reader feels the intensity of the scene and the rapid exchanges between the two women.

At other charged moments, Defoe's prose has considerable rhythm and beauty. After the death of Robin, Moll says, "I was resolv'd now to be Married, or Nothing, and to be well Married, or not at all." The balance in the sentence and the emphatic negatives emphasize her determination. Two years after the death of her last husband, Moll describes her situation as "driven by the dreadful Necessity of my Circumstances to the Gates of Destruction, Soul and Body; and two or three times I fell upon my Knees, praying to God, as well as I could, for Deliverance; but I cannot but say, my Prayers had no hope in them; I knew not what to do, it was all Fear without, and Dark within" (193). The sentence makes clear the pivotal moment in her life, and the resonance of "Soul and Body" makes clear that Moll faced more than starvation. Her very soul hung in the balance, and there was only "Fear without, and Dark within," another carefully balanced group of words placed for maximum evocative impact. Before another catastrophe, the time when the Colchester family is ready to put her out of the house, she says, "I saw the Cloud, tho' I did not foresee the Storm."

Although Defoe has sometimes been described as a writer who seldom uses metaphoric language, this is not so. Moll's consistent discussion of her career as a thief is in the language of trade and commerce, and other sections of the book draw specific parallels between Moll's activities and other aspects of life, as Moll's introduction into the art of the pickpocket draws upon the terms of midwifery. Moll often refers to herself as a commodity, and some of her metaphors make profound statements about woman's place in society: "when a Woman is thus left . . . void of Council, she is just like a Bag of Money, or a Jewel dropt on the Highway, which is a Prey to the next Comer." Some of the comparisons she uses to describe herself are horrifying in their confession of her manipulative and ruthless streak: "I play'd with this Lover, as an Angler does with a Trout."

As a young man Defoe had been devout enough to copy the entire Pentateuch when he feared that Nonconformists would be denied Bibles and to consider a career as a minister. Some of his most powerful images come from his deep familiarity with scriptural language. In Newgate, Moll says, "like the Waters in the Caveties, and Hollows of Mountains, which petrifies and turns into Stone whatever they are suffer'd to drop upon; so the continual Conversing with such a Crew of Hell-Hounds" turned her into "Stone . . . first Stupid and Senseless, then Brutish and thoughtless." In this passage the ring of the King James version of the Psalms adds emotional resonance. Much of his prose, even in a book for a readership like that of *Moll Flanders*, has an old-fashioned ring to it, reminiscent of the King James Bible or the books he had read as a child and young man. When the bank clerk dies, Moll writes, "a sudden Blow from an almost invisible Hand, blasted all my Happiness, and turn'd me out into the World in a Condition the reverse of all that had been before." Many of the books on Defoe's shelves frequently alluded to humankind's existence in a world fraught with unforeseeable events and governed by a plan beyond mortal understanding. Here, for example, is a passage from Richard Knolles' *Turkish History,* a book Defoe frequently quoted: "What small assurance there is in men's Affairs, and how subject unto change even those things are wherein we for the most part repose our greatest felicity and bliss." Such phrases conjure up the deeply resonant "O tempora mundi" themes in English literature and contribute to the readers' sympathy and excuses for Moll.

Even this highly rhetorical style is "realistic" for Moll. Given the time of her birth, the religious and historical beliefs of her actual contemporaries, her elevated references are really but the clichés abundantly used to explain the inexplicable. *Moll Flanders* was written, however, when such phrases were becoming unsatisfactory, and to a large extent the greatness of *Moll Flanders* comes from the way it communicates the breakdown of certainty, the tension between religious and secular modes of thought, and the acute awareness that "code ethics," whether biblical or national, were sometimes inadequate guides for conduct. Over and over, Moll Flanders recites the imperatives: the moral judgment and the practical reality. When she is faced with the older brother's insistence that she marry Robin and in a dozen subsequent episodes, she calls herself and the act by the harshest names in the Bible at the same moment that she depicts herself as being without options, trapped and desperate. At the time she marries Robin, for instance, she is his brother's "Whore" but also the "Bear [tied] to the Stake."

This complexity is carried over into the complexity of her character. Although she is one of the most dishonest characters in literature, one who seriously deceives (and to some extent injures) at least a half dozen men and who becomes a professional thief, she seems to be disclosing things that sane people would hide, confessing secret sins and the depravity of her soul. She is so memorable because she is so blunt and candid about her actions; if she is not "honest" about herself, it appears to be because she does not know herself fully. Yet she appears to be habitually, even pointlessly, addicted to lying, and the last scenes in the book emphasize both her secrets and her deceptiveness. She gives her son

Humphrey a stolen watch and makes sure that the reader knows; she lies to Jemy repeatedly about the source of her New World wealth, her family there, and her marriage to her brother, and she gives readers intricate summaries that assure her past will be fresh in their minds. She lies to Humphrey until time for the reunion. Her reasons for hiding many of these things seem practical and psychologically shrewd, but they complicate the interpretation of her character and throw in doubt her reliability as a narrator. At the same time, however, they illustrate the very human desire to make others think well of us and to avoid risking love and security. Moll eventually tells Jemy the truth, and his comment is like a benediction: "it was no Fault of yours; nor of his; it was a Mistake impossible to be prevented. . . . Thus all these little Difficulties were made easy; and we liv'd together with the greatest Kindness and Comfort imaginable; we are now grown Old" (342). This ending strengthens the division between act and actor, crime and human being, that animates so much of *Moll Flanders*. Jemy loves Moll, not in spite of her crimes, not "anyway," but because of what she is to him. Her incestuous marriage is irrelevant, and so the book ends with a final act of wish-fulfillment: Moll Flanders, without youth, beauty, or money, is lovable.

By the time Defoe wrote *Moll Flanders*, he had been a successful and prolific writer for more than thirty years. He had written more poetry than Milton, as well as periodicals, pamphlets, several histories, conduct books, short biographies, social and economic proposals, and fictional memoirs and journals. He had directed his writing to the nobility, to members of Parliament, to Scots (many of whom spoke a marked dialect), to women, and to the common people. His sentences had become a familiar, flexible instrument in his skilled hands. His works, *Moll Flanders* included, contain a large variety of sentence structures, several levels of diction, and a number of styles. Moll could give efficient, colloquial summaries, rise to emotional perorations in balanced, rhetorical sentences, or make short, cold statements. As George Starr has said about Defoe's fictional style in general,

Defoe renders things and events "*as* perceived, as in some sense transformed and recreated in the image of the narrator."[3] Even as he creates Moll's personality by the details he selects and by her reactions, he portrays her *Weltanschauung* vividly and strikingly fully. In doing so, he forces readers to evaluate Moll's perception of the world and how they interpret the world in which they themselves live.

CHAPTER 10

Enduring Questions

Moll Flanders has often been read as a powerful condemnation of Defoe's society, and especially of its materialism. In his lifetime, the national debt, the Bank of England, the stock market, and modern taxation came into existence, and money and credit replaced land and family as measures of power. What has been said of *Moll Flanders* could be said of his time; what matters is "the counting, measuring, pricing, weighing, and evaluating things in terms of the wealth they represent and the social status they imply for the possessor."[1] Whether seen as the reduction of an individual's existence to such concerns or as the texture of modern society, the idea is dehumanizing, and Moll does in fact try to renounce sentimentality, sensuality, and sympathy. She believes that those feelings that make her vulnerable must be repressed.

Moll's initiation into this society can be equated with an education in the significance of money, and money means independence, love, and respect. Without it, her home can be "swept away," she can be coerced into a loveless marriage she believes incestuous, she can be driven to commit crimes, and she can be insulted and ignored. She relinquishes her body to the older brother and learns that it is a commodity, a medium of exchange. She relinquishes her money to her second husband and quickly learns that she has, horribly and ironically, given up an even more effective medium of exchange. And then she nearly relinquishes her soul. She cuts these words on glass, "But Money's Vertue, Gold is Fate" (79). From the episodes in which she tricks men into marrying her through those in which her careful dress, gold watch, and gloves protect her from the suspicions and brutalities directed at other thieves, the deceiving, defining power of money remains consistent. She comes to associate it with her life blood, and several times remarks that "spending upon the main stock was but a certain kind of bleeding to death." It gives her courage and security; "with money in the pocket one is at home any where," she says cheerfully. Perhaps the most dreadful thing about her story is the pervasiveness of its power; it even saves her life and allows the fresh start in Virginia with Jemy. The message is simple: those without money live desperately and die miserably.

Defoe himself had painfully learned about money. He had been an imprisoned bankrupt and suffered the resulting hardships and insults for years. Without capital or credit, he had been forced into an occupation he would not have chosen, that of writer. About the time he wrote *Moll Flanders*, at age sixty-two, he tried to go back into trade and failed again. His nonfiction writing analyzed society and concentrated on economics, politics, and religion, and he had learned to see the power of money in global perspective. He had seen it win elections and wars. Over and over he wrote that the largest purse, not the longest sword, won wars, and he meant that wealth won modern wars. He could praise what England did with her wealth, but he often called money a drug and noted its addictive and stupefying effects. He could write passages that sound rather like hymns to money, but they almost never end on a note of praise.[2] Regardless of the ambiguity he expresses about money, he accepts its power and centrality to his society as a given.

Even if Moll could resist the materialistic and predatory nature of her world and those she meets in it, Defoe suggests she could not resist physical want. He consistently argued that people in situations they felt to be desperate could not be held responsible for the deplorable things they did.[3] He challenged people to withhold judgment unless they knew what they themselves would do by having been in the same situation. Statements in the *Review,* the periodical he wrote for nine years, reoccur in *Moll Flanders,* as this opinion does:

> Let the honestest Man in this Town tell me when he is sinking, when he sees his Family's Destruction in such an Arrest, or such a Seizure, and has his Friends Money by him, or has his Employers Effects in his Hand; Can he refrain from making use of it—? Can he forbear any more than a Starving Man will forbear his Neighbours Loaf? Will the honestest Man of you all, if ye were drowning in the *Thames,* refuse to lay hold of your Neighbour who is in the same Condition, for fear he drown with you? . . . What shall we say? —*Give me not Poverty, lest I Steal,* says the *Wiseman, that is,* if I am poor I shall be a thief; I tell you all, Gentlemen, in your Poverty, the best of you all will rob your Neighbour; nay go farther . . . you will not only rob your Neighbour, but if in distress, you will EAT your Neighbour, *ay,* and say Grace to your Meat too— Distress removes from the Soul, all Relation, Affection, Sense of Justice, and all the Obligations, either Moral or Religious, that secure one Man against another.
>
> Not that I say or suggest the Distress makes the Violence Lawful; but I say it is a Tryal beyond the Ordinary Power of Humane Nature to withstand. . . . (*Review,* 8:302)

> But there are Temptations which it is not in the Power of Human Nature to resist, and few know what would be their Case if driven to the same Exigences. As Covetousness is the Root of all Evil, so Poverty is . . . the worst of all Snares. (*Moll Flanders,* 188)

In later works, he repeats the idea. For instance, an anecdote in *Some Considerations upon Street-Walkers* [1726] is much like Moll's life. A prostitute explains that "Sir James" ruined her when she was a needy orphan. She became a prostitute and then a thief. She explains that the workhouse and whippings have not reformed her, for her "Wants threw me into my old Ways" (16–18). In this work, Defoe explains succinctly, "Man's Solicitation tempts them to Lewdness, Necessity succeeds Sin, and Want puts an End to Shame" (8).

Is society then to blame for Moll's depraved sensibility and her crimes? By emphasizing the pressures society exerts on individuals and by identifying some of its predominant forces, Defoe originated a major, essential aspect of the novel form and contributed a probing account of the relationship between personality and society. What Moll could resist is both a simple and more complex question than what she should have resisted. Quite simply, she obviously felt that she could resist none of the temptations to which she gave in, and Defoe often describes her as in a panicky, overwrought state at the moment she succumbs. Her hardheaded stock-taking, the tallying up of her economic gain, and the estimate of her spiritual loss all occur *after* the action. She does not anticipate gain, or imagine the coins, cloth, or jewelry she will get; she acts emotionally. The alternatives to the action, not the benefits, motivate her. Yet, the question is infinitely complex and cuts to the very heart of Defoe's art, for, like the tolerance for pain, each individual's ability to resist is somewhat different, even as it falls between fairly clear universal human limits. And so the questions arise: Does she resist enough? Should Defoe have made her resist more? Is her resistance immorally low or is it about normal?

Yet another aspect of the relationship Defoe sets up between the individual and society is destructive, and here Defoe's decision to use a heroine pays full measure. In the eighteenth century a woman's life was laid out for her, and expectations for her were narrow indeed. Moll rejects the life that is her destiny, and Defoe was well aware that many would consider that alone a sin, a rebellion against natural order. And so a life-and-death struggle begins between the individual who wanted to live, in George Eliot's words, "the life that was in her," and the social elements that worked in concert to keep her in her place.

Moll believes herself too good to be a servant. In the Colchester family, she demonstrates that she has every attribute and talent desired in a wife—except money. Her long life is a history of superior ingenuity, resilience, and courage. All around her people give up and die. The Mint is full of wretches who despair, drink themselves into a stupor, spend their last farthing, and repeat the pattern the next day. Men go bankrupt and die of broken hearts. Her brother sinks into madness. Thieves take desperate chances and are caught and hanged. Newgate reduces them all to mindless suffering. Except for brief periods, the most threatening in Newgate, Moll refuses to give in. She surveys her shattered life and begins anew with hardly a glance behind her.

Moll wants a better life than the one society has determined for her, and she wants independence. Perhaps the most frustrating thing patriarchal society does to women, the poor, and the different is to deny them adulthood. It wants to manage their money and tell them what to do, think, and be. Even the good bank clerk says to Moll suggestively, "Why do you not get a head Steward, Madam, that may take you and your Money together into keeping, and then you would have the trouble taken off of your Hands?" "Ay Sir, and the Money too, it may be," she answers (132). Moll soon comes to appreciate the value of acquiring and managing her own money. She learns that it gives her status and protection. With a private stock she can avoid the whims, weaknesses, and misfortunes of her husbands, and she can be prepared to deal with disasters. When the cost of a pardon would dangerously deplete her savings, she wisely chooses transportation. For such people to establish independence, however, there must be acts of rebellion, and Moll often resists advice, and even orders, vehemently. She perverts the purposes and sacred nature of marriage, and she becomes, in fact, what she represents, for theft is a rebellion against society and a crime against order. She violates a number of basic social principles including respect for the ownership of property and trust among members of a community; criminals always want to live by their own laws and fulfill their own desires.

She asserts the supreme importance of her desires, her ambitions, and her personality. One interpretation presents Moll in a dialectic of power with the Other, which is identified as society, history, and circumstance.[4] It goes beyond the story to argue that the book proves the power of the individual to determine reality. Not only does Moll avoid her destiny repeatedly and achieve her independence, her "reality," but Defoe draws his readers into her world and forces us to confront her uncomfortable questions and her reality. Because her desires are so perfectly ordinary and yet accomplished in such completely unacceptable ways, she stands for the universal human aspiration for dignity and independence—adulthood—in an unsympathetic world. But is egoism such as hers evil? Can personality be denied?

Thus, *Moll Flanders* raises yet another set of questions, which can be summarized simply: What is evil? What is its source? Of what are we capable? Who can forget Moll's rising series of questions to the unfeeling older brother and his callous jokes about her? Or the arresting, dreadful moment when Moll says, "Here, I say, the Devil put me upon killing the Child in the dark Alley, that it might not Cry, but the very thought frighted me so that I was ready to drop down" (194)? Or the completely neutral way she slips part of the coins she has won in her pocket as she pretends indifference to winning, amusement at the game, and finally gratitude to the man who has staked her? Or the moment she says of the news that one of her confederates was hanged, "at last she sent me the joyful News that he was hang'd, which was the best News to me that I had heard a great while" (219–20)? And who can forget the child who watches her nurse's house "swept away," the young woman who hears her lover tell her that he will see that she is turned out, penniless, on the road, or the woman, who after yet another disappointment, walks the streets of London feeling her decreasing savings to be a gradual loss of her own blood? At first we wonder what Moll Flanders will do next, but we come to wonder and continue to wonder what kind of person she is. What is the relation between good and evil in a person's life? Can both exist in the same person? Is the person good or evil, or just the person's words or actions? And what are the evidences of evil? Are thoughts without actions evil (Moll's impulse to kill the child)? Are actions without knowledge (Moll's marriage to her brother)?

What is evil? Is it part of human nature, as basic as hunger or thirst? Is it a misperception of the world—for instance, a focus on self instead of God? Is it a person's twisted response to overpowering forces? How does evil grow within a human heart? Does it feed on itself, increasing because it satisfies human wants? Does it grow because impulses toward good are attenuated? Why do the "evils" in a society, such as ignorance and want, result in moral evil for the ignorant and wanting? Defoe makes judgment difficult and teases us into engaging yet again eternal questions that each of us must finally take responsibility for answering for ourselves.

Notes

1. Historical Context

1. Gerald Howson, "Who Was Moll Flanders?" *TLS* 67:1 (18 January 1968): 63–64.

2. *The Fortunes and Misfortunes of the Famous Moll Flanders,* ed. G. A. Starr (London: Oxford University Press, 1971), 1, 4. All quotations are from this edition.

2. The Importance of the Work

1. Anthony Burgess, "Modern Novels: The 99 Best," *New York Times Book Review,* 5 February, 1984, 36–37.

3. Critical Reception

1. J. L. Wood, "Defoe Serialized," *Factotum: Newsletter of the XVIIth Century STC* 19 (1984): 21–23.

2. John Bender, *Imagining the Penitentiary: Fiction and the Architecture of Mind in Eighteenth-Century England* (Chicago: University of Chicago Press, 1987), 43–44.

3. Starr, Introduction to *The Fortunes and Misfortunes of the Famous Moll Flanders,* xvi–xvii.

4. *Review* in *Defoe's Review,* ed. Arthur W. Secord, 22 vols. (New York: Columbia University Press, 1938), 7:65. All quotations from the *Review* are from this facsimile edition.

5. George Chalmers, *The Life of Daniel De Foe* (London, 1790), 59.

6. Quoted in Pat Rogers, ed., *Defoe: The Critical Heritage* (London:

Routledge & Kegan Paul, 1972), 93, and in Alan D. McKillop, *The Early Masters of English Fiction* (Lawrence: University of Kansas Press, 1956), 33, respectively. Other surveys of the critical reception of *Moll Flanders* are in Rogers; in J. Paul Hunter, ed., *Moll Flanders* (New York: Crowell, 1970), xix–xx, 271–76; and in Ian Watt, "The Recent Critical Fortunes of *Moll Flanders,*" *Eighteenth-Century Studies* 1 (1967): 109–26.

7. Virginia Woolf, *The Common Reader* (New York: Harcourt, Brace & Company, 1925), 127.

8. William Faulkner, "To the Book Editor of the *Chicago Tribune,*" in *Essays, Speeches, and Public Letters by William Faulkner,* ed. James B. Meriwether (New York: Random House, 1965), 198.

4. Story and Structure

1. E. M. Forster, *Aspects of the Novel* (New York: Harcourt, Brace, 1927), 215.

2. G. A. Starr, *Defoe and Spiritual Autobiography* (Princeton: Princeton University Press, 1965), 137.

3. Lincoln B. Faller, *Turned to Account* (Cambridge: Cambridge University Press, 1987), 166–67, 196.

4. Bender, *Imagining the Penitentiary,* 46–47.

5. Setting

1. *A Tour Thro' the Whole Island of Great Britain,* 2 vols. (London: Dent, 1962), 1:314.

2. *Serious Reflections during the Life and Strange Adventures of Robinson Crusoe,* ed. G. H. Maynadier (New York: The C. T. Brainard Publishing Co., 1903), 4, 6.

3. Patricia Meyer Spacks, "Women and the City," in *Johnson and His Age,* ed. James Engell (Cambridge, Mass. Harvard English Studies 12, 1984), 485–90.

4. Adrienne Rich, "Teaching Language in Open Admissions," in *On Lies, Secrets, and Silence* (New York: Norton, 1979), 54.

5. *Colonel Jack,* 2 vols., Shakespeare Head Edition (London: Blackwell, 1927–28), 1:207.

6. Moll, the Criminal

1. Frank W. Chandler, *The Literature of Roguery* (Boston: Houghton, Mifflin, 1907), 64–65.

2. Faller, *Turned to Account,* 91. The quotation from Talbot is on this page too.

3. See, for example, Maximillian E. Novak, *Defoe and the Nature of Man* (London: Oxford University Press, 1963).

4. Faller, *Turned to Account,* 29, 228–29 n.7.

5. British Library Loan 29/369, letters from j.p's for 27 and 28 February 170$\frac{4}{3}$.

6. J. M. Beattie, *Crime and the Courts in England, 1660–1800* (Princeton: Princeton University Press, 1986), 470–83.

7. Roger Morrice, "The Entring Book," 28 November 1682, 1:346. Information in this chapter is from Beattie, *Crime and the Courts in England;* Abbott Smith, *Colonists in Bondage* (Chapel Hill: University of North Carolina Press, 1947); and David W. Galenson, *White Servitude in Colonial America: An Economic Analysis* (Cambridge: Cambridge University Press, 1981).

8. Beattie, *Crime and the Courts in England,* 504–5; Smith, *Colonists in Bondage,* 110–25.

9. Beattie, *Crime and the Courts in England,* 454–70, passim; Smith, *Colonists in Bondage,* 91–92, 128–29.

10. Smith, *Colonists in Bondage,* 254–57, 303–5.

11. *Plan of the English Commerce* (London, 1728), 228–29; *Atlas Maritimus* (London, 1728), 325–31; *General History of Discoveries and Improvements* (London, 1727), 287–98.

7. Moll, Romantic Narrator

1. William H. Gass, "The Concept of Character in Fiction," in *Essentials of the Theory of Fiction,* eds. Michael Hoffman and Patrick Murphy (Durham, N.C.: Duke University Press, 1988), 268.

2. See Howard L. Koonce, "Moll's Muddle: Defoe's Use of Irony in *Moll Flanders,*" *ELH* 30 (1963): 377–88.

3. See David Blewitt, *Defoe's Art of Fiction* (Toronto: University of Toronto Press, 1979), 55, and Everett Zimmerman, *Defoe and the Novel* (Berkeley: University of California Press, 1975), 105–6.

4. Zimmerman, *Defoe and the Novel*, 106.

5. See G. A. Starr's fine description of the way Moll gains reader sympathy, *Defoe and Casuistry* (Princeton: Princeton University Press, 1971), chapter 4.

6. E. P. Thompson, *The Making of the English Working Class* (1963; Harmondsworth, England: Penguin, 1984), 367–69; Margaret Spufford, "First Steps in Literacy," *Social History* 4 (1979): 413–15; Alan MacFarlane, *Marriage and Love in England* (Oxford: Blackwell, 1986), 75–76.

7. David Blewitt, "Changing Attitudes toward Marriage in the Time of Defoe: The Case of *Moll Flanders*," *HLQ* 44 (1981): 77–88.

8. Chandler, *The Literature of Roguery*, 292.

8. Minor Characters

1. John Masefield, "Daniel Defoe," *Fortnightly Review*, 1 January 1909, 72.

2. See Robert A. Erickson, *Mother Midnight*, (New York: AMS Press, 1986), especially parts 1 and 2.

3. Ibid., 56–64.

4. Faller, *Turned to Account*, 6–20, 118–24, 174–93.

5. B. L., *An Accurate Description of Newgate* (London, 1729), 45.

9. Language and Style

1. P. N. Furbank and W. R. Owens, *The Canonisation of Daniel Defoe* (New Haven, Conn.: Yale University Press, 1988), 130.

2. G. A. Starr, "Defoe's Prose Style: 1. The Language of Interpretation," *Modern Philology* 71 (1974): 290.

3. Ibid., 281.

10. Enduring Questions

1. Compare Dorothy Van Ghent, *The English Novel: Form and Function* (New York: Holt, Rinehart & Winston, 1953), 35, and Bender, *Imagining the Penitentiary*, 58.

2. Cf. *Review* 3:15–16; 4:422–24.

Notes

3. The most detailed discussion of this idea is in Novak's *Defoe and the Nature of Man,* 78–87, passim.

4. John Richetti, *Defoe's Narratives* (Oxford: Clarendon, 1975), chapter 4.

Selected Bibliography

Primary Works

There is no collected edition of Defoe's works. The best, the Shakespeare Head Edition, *Novels and Selected Writings of Daniel Defoe,* in fourteen volumes (Oxford: Blackwell, 1927–28), is available in reprint editions. Most of the works attributed to Defoe are available in the University Microfilm, Great Britain, series. The best modern editions of *The Fortunes and Misfortunes of the Famous Moll Flanders* that are still in print are the Oxford University Press edition (1971; ed. G. A. Starr) and the Penguin Classic (1989; ed. David Blewitt). The Norton Critical Edition (1973; ed. Edward Kelly) and the Houghton Mifflin Riverside edition (1959; ed. James Sutherland) are acceptable teaching editions, although Sutherland reprints the less desirable, shorter third edition.

Books

The following is an extremely selective list of Defoe's works. The reader should consult the *New Cambridge Bibliography,* ed. George Watson, 2: 880–917 (Cambridge: Cambridge University Press, 1971).

Reflections upon the Late Great Revolution. London, 1689.

An Essay upon Projects. London, 1697.

The Poor Man's Plea for a Reformation of Manners and Suppressing Immorality in the Nation. London, 1698.

The True-Born Englishman: A Satyr. London, 1700.

[Legion's Memorial]. [London, 1701].

Selected Bibliography

The History of the Kentish Petition. London, 1701.

The Original Power of the Collective Body of the People of England, Examined and Asserted. London, 1702.

The Shortest Way with the Dissenters. London, 1702.

A Hymn to the Pillory. London, 1703.

The Consolidator. London, 1705.

An Essay at Removing National Prejudices against a Union with Scotland. London, 1706.

Jure Divino: A Satyr in Twelve Books. London, 1706.

Caledonia: A Poem in Honour of Scotland, and the Scots Nation. London, 1706.

A Brief History of the Poor Palatine Refugees. London, 1709.

The History of the Union of Great Britain. Edinburgh, 1709.

An Essay upon Publick Credit. London, 1710.

Reasons Why This Nation Ought to Put a Speedy End to This Expensive War. London, 1711.

An Essay on the History of Parties, and Persecution in Britain. London, 1711.

The Present State of the Parties in Great Britain. London, 1712.

And What if the Pretender Should Come. London, 1711.

A General History of Trade. 4 pts. London, 1713.

Memoirs of Count Tariff. London, 1713.

Memoirs of John Duke of Melfort. London, 1714.

The Secret History of the White Staff: Being an Account of Affairs under the Conduct of Some Late Ministers. London, 1714.

Advice to the People of Great Britain. London, 1714.

The Fears of the Pretender Turn'd into the Fears of Debauchery. London, 1715.

An Appeal to Honour and Justice. London, 1715.

The Family Instructor, in Three Parts. London, 1715.

An Account of the Conduct of Robert Earl of Oxford. London, 1715.

Fair Payment No Spunge: Or Some Considerations on the Unreasonableness of Refusing to Receive Back Money Lent on Publick Securities. London, 1717.

The Question Fairly Stated, Whether Now is Not the Time to do Justice to the Friends of the Government as well as to its Enemies. London, 1717.

Considerations on the Present State of Affairs in Great-Britain. London, 1718.

Memoirs of the Life and Eminent Conduct of that Learned and Reverend Divine Daniel Williams DD. London, 1718.

Memoirs of Publick Transactions in the Life and Ministry of his Grace the D. of Shrewsbury. London, 1718.

A Continuation of Letters Written by a Turkish Spy at Paris. London, 1718.

The Memoirs of Majr Alexander Ramkins. London, 1719.

The Life and Strange Surprizing Adventures of Robinson Crusoe. London, 1719.

The Anatomy of Exchange-Alley: Or a System of Stock-Jobbing. London, 1719.

The Farther Adventures of Robinson Crusoe. London, 1719.

A Brief State of the Question, Between the Printed and Painted Callicoes and the Woollen and Silk Manufacture. London, 1719.

The King of Pirates: Being an Account of the Famous Enterprises of Captain Avery. London, 1720.

Memoirs of a Cavalier. London, [1720].

The Life, Adventures and Pyracies of the Famous Captain Singleton. London, 1720.

Serious Reflections during the Life and Surprising Adventures of Robinson Crusoe. London, 1720.

The South-Sea Scheme Examin'd. London, 1720.

The Fortunes and Misfortunes of the Famous Moll Flanders. London, 1721.

Due Preparations for the Plague as Well for Soul as Body. London, 1722.

Religious Courtship. London, 1722.

A Journal of the Plague Year. London, 1722.

The History and Remarkable Life of the Truly Honourable Col. Jacque. London, 1723.

The Fortunate Mistress. London, 1724.

The Great Law of Subordination Consider'd. London, 1724.

A Tour Thro' the Whole Island of Great Britain. London, 1724–27.

A Narrative of All the Robberies, Escapes etc of John Sheppard. London, 1724.

The Complete English Tradesman. 2 vols. London, 1725–27.

A General History of Discoveries and Improvements. 4 pts. London, 1725–26.

The Political History of the Devil. London, 1726.

The Protestant Monastery: or a Complaint against the Brutality of the Present Age. London, 1727.

A System of Magick. London, 1727.

Conjugal Lewdness: or Matrimonial Whoredom. London, 1727.

A Brief Deduction of the Original, Progress and Immense Greatness of the British Woolen Manufacture. London, 1727.

An Essay on the History and Reality of Apparitions. London, 1727.

A New Family Instructor, In Familiar Discourses between a Father and his Children. London, 1727.

Augusta Triumphans: Or the Way to Make London the Most Flourishing City in the Universe. London, 1728.

A Plan of the English Commerce. London, 1728.

Atlas Maritimus and Commercialis: Or a General View of the World, so far as it relates to Trade and Navigation. London, 1728.

The Compleat English Gentleman, edited by Karl Bülbring. London, 1890.

Secondary Works

Biography

Backscheider, Paula R. *Daniel Defoe: His Life.* Baltimore: The Johns Hopkins University Press, 1989.

Bastian, Frank. *The Early Life of Daniel Defoe.* London: Macmillan, 1981.

Moore, John Robert. *Daniel Defoe: Citizen of the Modern World.* Bloomington: Indiana University Press, 1958.

Sutherland, James. *Defoe.* London: Methuen, 1937; rev. ed., 1950.

Critical Studies: Books

Alkon, Paul. *Defoe and Fictional Time.* Athens: University of Georgia Press, 1979. A theoretical study of time concepts in Defoe's novels including a sophisticated discussion of fictional time.

Backscheider, Paula R. *A Being More Intense.* New York: AMS Press, 1984. A consideration of Bunyan, Swift, and Defoe that finds the origins of the major directions that novelistic character creation would take.

————. *Daniel Defoe: Ambition and Innovation.* Lexington: University Press of Kentucky, 1986. A discussion of all of Defoe's writings, that points out how Defoe combined genres for maximum audience appeal.

Bell, Ian A. *Defoe's Fiction.* Totowa, N.J.: Barnes & Noble Books, 1985. A survey of Defoe's work as popular literature, which sees *Moll Flanders* as a sign of Defoe's developing ability to deal with states of mind and individual consciousnesses.

Bender, John. *Imagining the Penitentiary.* Chicago: University of Chicago Press, 1987. Argues that the novel is an ideological and historical document that participates in social change, noting specifically that books like *Moll Flanders* are cultural symbols that help shape institutions like prisons.

Blewitt, David. *Defoe's Art of Fiction.* Toronto: University of Toronto Press, 1979. Sees *Moll Flanders* as an important step in Defoe's development as a creative artist and indicative of his growing pessimism about human nature.

Erickson, Robert A. *Mother Midnight.* New York: AMS Press, 1986. Explores the contemporary myths surrounding the Mother Midnight figures represented in eighteenth-century fiction.

McKillop, Alan D. *The Early Masters of English Fiction.* Lawrence: University of Kansas Press, 1968. One of the first major modern studies of Defoe's place in the history of the novel.

Novak, Maximillian E. *Defoe and the Nature of Man.* London: Oxford University Press, 1963. A study of Defoe's attitude toward the laws of nature.

————. *Realism, Myth, and History in Defoe's Fiction.* Lincoln: Nebraska University Press, 1983. A collection of fine, somewhat revised essays elucidating some of the subtleties of Defoe's fictional art.

Richetti, John, *Defoe's Narratives: Situations and Structures.* Oxford: Clarendon Press, 1975. A sophisticated interpretation of the ways Defoe represented tensions between the individual and society and between cultural forces in his fiction.

Rogers, Pat, ed. *Defoe: The Critical Heritage* London: Routledge, 1972. A survey of critical reactions to Defoe's work.

————. *Literature and Popular Culture in Eighteenth-Century England.* Totowa, N.J.: Barnes & Noble, 1985. Includes a chapter on chapbook editions of *Moll Flanders*.

Starr, G. A. *Defoe and Casuistry.* Princeton: Princeton University Press, 1971. Points out Defoe's debt to the "cases of conscience" literature with a valuable chapter on the ways *Moll Flanders* approaches some vexed ethical problems.

————. *Defoe and Spiritual Autobiography.* Princeton: Princeton University Press, 1965. Explains the spiritual autobiography form and tests Defoe's novels against it in order to discuss Defoe's originality and to interpret his themes.

Watt, Ian. *The Rise of the Novel.* Berkeley: University of California Press, 1975. The classic study of the merging of the rise of the middle class, economic individualism, and the novel.

Weinstein, Arnold. *Fictions of the Self: 1550–1800.* Princeton: Princeton University Press, 1981. Discusses Moll Flanders as a great character, an "authentic," fully realized literary creation.

Zimmerman, Everett. *Defoe and the Novel.* Berkeley: University of California Press, 1975. Explains how Defoe's technique as a novelist improves with experience. Zimmerman sees the "editor" of the novel giving an important third perspective.

Critical Studies: Articles

Alter, Robert. "A Bourgeois Picaroon." In *Rogue's Progress: Studies in the Picaresque Novel,* 35–57. Harvard Studies in Comparative Literature, 26. Cambridge, Mass.: Harvard University Press, 1964. Concludes from sound reasons that *Moll Flanders* is not a picaresque novel.

Backscheider, Paula R. "Defoe's Women: Snares and Prey." *Studies in Eighteenth-Century Culture* 5 (1976): 103–20. Important to meaning and to moral complexity is the fact that Moll Flanders is both snare and prey.

Blewitt, David. "Changing Attitudes toward Marriage in the Time of Defoe: The Case of Moll Flanders." *Huntington Library Quarterly* 44 (1981): 77–88. Demonstrates how Defoe used the opinions of

William Fleetwood and others in his novels and how these ideas differed from earlier attitudes toward children and marriage.

Braudy, Leo. "Daniel Defoe and the Anxieties of Autobiography." *Genre* 6 (1973): 76–97. A pioneering study of the ways Defoe's characters express threats to personality and personal identity.

Brown, Homer O. "The Displaced Self in the Novels of Daniel Defoe." *English Literary History* 38 (1971): 562–90. Defoe's characters simultaneously and compulsively disguise and conceal their essential selves.

Joyce, James. "Daniel Defoe." *Buffalo Studies* 1 (1964): 5–27. An appreciation of Defoe's realistic style.

Karl, Frederick R. "Moll's Many-Colored Coat: Veil and Disguise in the Fiction of Defoe." *Studies in the Novel* 5 (1973): 86–97. Defoe employes disguises and other strategies to show characters, including Moll Flanders, trying to reshape their lives and thereby accommodate themselves to social change.

Kettle, Arnold. "In Defence of 'Moll Flanders.'" In *Of Books and Humankind.* ed. John Butt. (London: Routledge and Kegan Paul, 1964):55–67. Moll Flanders expresses the universal human aspiration for independence, but Newgate Prison finally reduces her to a conformist.

Peterson, Spiro. "The Matrimonial Theme of Defoe's *Roxana.*" *PMLA* 70 (1955): 166–91. *Moll Flanders* and *Roxana* develop themes critical of contemporary marriage and divorce laws.

Pollack, Ellen. "*Moll Flanders,* Incest, and the Structures of Exchange." *The Eighteenth Century: Theory and Interpretation* 30 (1989): 3–21.

Rader, Ralph. "Defoe, Richardson, Joyce, and the Concept of Form in the Novel." In *Autobiography, Biography, and the Novel: Papers Read at a Clark Library Seminar.* Berkeley: University of California Press, 1973. Uses *Moll Flanders* to define Defoe's novel form as "simulated naive incoherent autobiography," a strategy that contributed to the illusion of a genuine account.

Starr, G. A. "Defoe's Prose Style: 1. The Language of Interpretation." *Modern Philology* 71 (1974): 277–94. An intelligent essay on Defoe's strategies for rendering subjectivity of perception and interpretation.

Index

Alkon, Paul, 15
Applebee's Journal, 2
Arnold, Matthew, 16
Aubin, Penelope: *Life of Madame de Beaumont,* 4
Austen, Jane, 61

Backscheider, Paula R., 15–16
Bakhtin, Mikhail, 16
Behn, Aphra, 65, 83
Bell, Ian, 15
Bender, John, 10, 17, 27, 38
Bible, 59, 89, 90
Black Act, 2
Blewitt, David, 15
Bunyan, John, 43; *Pilgrim's Progress,* 7, 82–83
Burgess, Anthony, 8

Chalmers, George, 12
colonization, 1, 52, 54–55, 79
comedy, 28
conduct books, 3
Crane, Stephen, 57–58
crime, 1–3, 8, 48, 80; literature of, 2–3, 10, 16, 23–24, 27, 40–44, 47, 55, 66–67

criminals, 21–22, 26, 41, 47–49, 55, 67, 80–81, 98; highwaymen, 78, 87
Cross, Wilbur, 14
Culler, Jonathan, 16

DEFOE, Daniel. life, 1–3, 32–33, 55, 66–67, 83, 89–90, 91–92, 94; love of language games, 28, 76; opinions of, 1, 11, 30, 53–55, 70, 94; popularity of fiction, 10–11

WORKS: FICTION
Captain Singleton, 14
Colonel Jack, 1, 13, 14, 30, 38, 47, 49–53, 74
Journal of the Plague Year, 11, 13, 17
Memoirs of a Cavalier, 13
Robinson Crusoe, 1, 3, 6, 7, 13–14, 17, 28, 34, 83
Roxana, 13–14

WORKS: NONFICTION
25, 30, 46, 53–54, 73–74
Atlas Maritimus, 52, 53
Augusta Triumphans, 70
Conjugal Lewdness, 66

About the Author

Paula R. Backscheider is professor of English at the University of Rochester. She is author of two critical books, *A Being More Intense: The Prose Works of Bunyan, Swift, and Defoe* and *Daniel Defoe: Ambition and Innovation,* and a biography, *Daniel Defoe: His Life.* In addition, she has edited *Probability, Time, and Space in Eighteenth-Century Literature,* the plays of Elizabeth Inchbald and of Samuel Foote, the Garland eighteenth-century drama series, the English books part of *The Eighteenth Century: A Current Bibliography,* and the three-volume *Dictionary of Literary Biography: Restoration and Eighteenth-Century Drama.* Her articles have appeared in *PMLA, ELH, Modern Language Review, Modern Philology, Philological Quarterly,* and numerous other journals. A member of the Institute for Advanced Studies in the Humanities, University of Edinburgh, she has held ACLS, NEH, Mellon, and American Philosophical Society fellowships.